D0458352

JIM NORTON

Happy Endings

THE TALES OF A MEATY-BREASTED ZILCH

SIMON SPOTLIGHT ENTERTAINMENT
NEW YORK LONDON TORONTO SYDNEY

SIMON SPOTLIGHT ENTERTAINMENT
An imprint of Simon & Schuster
1230 Avenue of the Americas, New York, New York 10020
SIMON SPOTLIGHT ENTERTAINMENT and related logo are trademarks of
Simon & Schuster, Inc.
Designed by Purple Gate Design
Photograph on page 20 is courtesy of Andrew Swank and WYSP
Manufactured in the United States of America

10 9 8 7 6 5 4 3 2
Library of Congress Cataloging-in-Publication Data
Norton, Jim, 1968-
Happy endings / by Jim Norton. — 1st ed.
p. cm.
ISBN-13: 978-1-4169-5022-6
ISBN-10: 1-4169-5022-2
1. Norton, Jim, 1968- 2. Comedians—United States—Biography.
3.Radio personalities—United States—Biography. I. Title.
PN2287.N574A3 2007
792.702'8092—dc22
[B]
2007010641

CONTENTS

FOREWORD BY COLIN QUINN   1
FOREWORD BY COLIN QUINN: PART TWO   3
A TRULY PROFESSIONAL INTRODUCTION   5
HERE GOES NOTHING   11
RUMPLESTILTSKIN   13
THE MASSAGE   17
MORBID OBESITY   19
LAS VEGAS   25
SITCOMS   28
A ROAD STORY   33
I'M A POET AND DIDN'T KNOW IT   39
PINK EYE   49
COINS   51
THE BIG COLLECTION   53
BOO!   57
1987 LETTER I WROTE TO A GIRL I WAS DATING   63
JOE PESKY   69
ANOTHER SILLY SITCOM IDEA   71
PUMPKIN, A LOVE STORY   75
SLEEPY HEAD   83
36   87
HAPPY HUMP DAY!   93
THE BOB LEVY BENEFIT   97
THE GREATEST MOMENT OF MY LIFE   103
MILF   107
LEGAL EAGLES   111
THE HOLLAND TUNNEL   115

THE DUMP WHISPERER   119

CURRENTLY IN BRAZIL   121

I'D LOVE TO LIVE IN RIO   125

TOUGH CROWD   133

COUCH POTATER   141

THE VOYEUR BUS   145

AN ENCHANTING EVENING   151

1986 NOTE I GOT FROM AN EX-GIRLFRIEND   155

"GLENGARRY GLEN ROSS" AND THE SEARCH FOR HAWKEYE   159

THE JACUZZI BLUES   171

DIRK   177

A DISASTER MOVIE! PART 1   183

HAPPY BIRTHDAY, DEAR FLORENTINE   187

YOU GELLIN'?   193

KONG   197

MONSTER RAIN   203

LITTLE MISS BIG NIPS   207

AN UNEVENTFUL, SHITTY NIGHT IN BOSTON   209

THE TWO-FOOT RULE   213

YUCK MOUTH   215

MEAN GENE THE HUGGING MACHINE   219

ROACHES FOR THE BEST MAN   227

ACKNOWLEDGMENTS   234

WARNING

IF YOU ARE EASILY OFFENDED BY HUMOR, PLEASE FUCK OFF AND
BUY SOMETHING ELSE. ANY E-MAILS NOT FILLED WITH PRAISE
AND/OR OFFERS FOR A SLOPPY BLOWJOB WILL BE DELETED.

JIM NORTON
APRIL 2007

For Jade
You were a great friend, a great roommate,
and your farts were atrocious.
I wish you could have stayed a little longer.
Love, Jim

FOREWORD BY COLIN QUINN

JIM NORTON IS an ass. When he asked me to write this foreword to his book, he, of course, never thought to send me the book itself because he doesn't read books and doesn't realize that the foreword is supposed to have a part where the person says this book is one of the funniest . . . it resonates . . . it's a fresh voice on the literary scene. He's such an ass that he probably thinks the foreword is like a comedy club introduction; as the MC of his fucking book I just write: Ladies and gentlemen, please enjoy the comedy stylings of a true comic genius, Jim Norton.

Jim Norton is one of the great ones in comedy and he's only started. The way he writes and the way his mind works is original, intelligent, and most important, always as funny as anyone I've seen.

One of the times when Jim Norton was on *Tough Crowd*, I mentioned to the panel of comics that the Olsen twins had been in a movie where they went to Europe, and Jim Norton yelled out, "*Passport to Paris*, stupid!" Another time we were in the greenroom at the show waiting to go on, and there was some comic who was from California. He didn't know Jim, and he was talking about a movie or TV show or something that he was working on. Whatever it was, his upbeat attitude was aggravating Jim. So, of course, Jim asked him a question that required a long answer, and as the guy started responding Jim nodded like he was interested and pushed the door so it closed in the guy's face midsentence.

Now, that would be obnoxious if Jim Norton was a physical entity. But Jim is a self-described "fat-titted nothing," so that changes the stakes and makes it ten times funnier when he stands up against the mediocrity in all of us, and especially in himself. That is why he's so funny. Jim Norton never says "People that do that," if he's done it or does it or is thinking about doing it. To describe Jim as "dirty" or "shocking" is to miss the point. He's not trying to be dirty or shocking. He's revealing himself, warts and all, and whether he's talking about his awful acting or his uncomfortable sexual encounters it's always in the interest of being funny and honest.

So what can I say, except . . . ladies and gentlemen, please enjoy the comedy stylings of a true comic genius, Jim Norton.

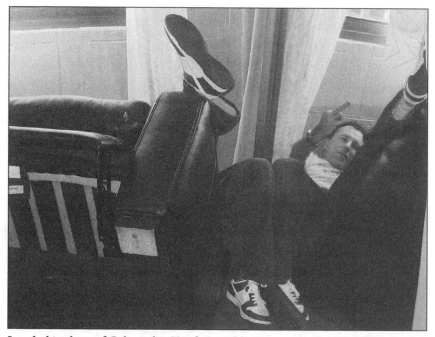

I took this photo of Colin in his *Tough Crowd* dressing room after his chair tipped over. But *I'm* an ass.

FOREWORD BY COLIN QUINN: PART TWO

My new foreword, since I just read the whole fucking thing

I HAVE JUST finished reading Jim Norton's new book a day after I received my second Lasik eye surgery. I mention this not just because I am finished to the point where I've had two Lasik surgeries, but because the fact that I shouldn't be straining my eyes to support a friend means nothing to Jim, as long as his book comes in on time. So I sat here all day and I have to be honest, I could not stop laughing. This ass has really written a hilarious and unpitying look at his awful, sex-addicted life. In addition, there are many heartwarming chapters of his teen years, including several secret documents that he has uncovered in the form of awful poetry and cowardly self-interested love letters. But you have to give credit to a man who is so brutally self-analyzing that he even questions the sincerity of his own suicide attempt.

This book is really hilarious. Even if it wasn't I would probably say it was because I feel important being asked to write a foreword for a book, but I swear to you, you will never read an autobiography like this. It's obscene, profane, intelligent, depressing, Godless, and hopeful. When God made Jim Norton he broke the mold. Or when God broke the mold he made Jim Norton. Please enjoy this work of comic brilliance. Or don't. Honestly, I am not that invested in the success of this one way or the other.

Love, Colin

A TRULY PROFESSIONAL INTRODUCTION

I HAVE NO fucking idea where to start. I'm supposed to write a proposal for this stupid book, but no one has told me what that entails. Should I be melodramatic and talk about the mortality rate of children under six in Third World countries? Or should the tone be breezy and whimsical, perhaps an anecdote about spilling a semen sample on my tie? Either way I win, I suppose; I love whimsy and hate children.

I had lunch this afternoon with Lydia, my potential literary agent. We met in a place on Forty-fourth Street in Manhattan at noon, which is still horribly early for a Saturday. I pried myself out of bed about eleven fifteen, all groggy, and sat stupidly in front of the computer until it was time to leave. Last night I took some cold medicine to help me sleep and now I feel hungover and shitty. We were brought to a table next to three fat businesswomen who were laughing and prattling on about nothing. And not only are these blathering fatsos having the time of their lives, they're doing it loudly. My head hurts and my fucking sinuses are blocked; I really want to pick up a baseball bat and smash one of their heads on the table like DeNiro in *The Untouchables*. A nice solid CLUNK, the sound of a coconut being split open, followed by blood and brains all over the table and a stunned, uncomfortable silence. Since I am basically a coward and can never find a bat when I need one, I enjoyed that thought for a few moments and giggled good-naturedly.

I tend to be incredibly awkward at these lunches, and the fact that Lydia is very attractive doesn't help. Attempting to idiotically flirt with her is out of the question, as she is married to a 6'4" martial artist. Not to

5

mention that as we're talking I'm coughing and literally have snot leaking out of my nose. We must be an enchanting sight: the hot blonde and the leaky nosed, unshaven fat neck in the Comedy Cellar T-shirt. After about ten minutes of mindless prattle from the sea lions at the next table, a tan, bisexual waiter sashays over to take our orders. We both get crab salads, which come in portions that a Somalian would laugh at. After finishing our shitty, two-bite lunch, we began to talk about me possibly writing a book of some sort.

When I refer to Lydia as my potential literary agent, I say "potential" not in reference to her willingness to work together, but in reference to my complete laziness. I love to write but I don't do it often because I am such a quick-fix junkie. I need a reaction *now*. One of the more satisfying things about stand-up is that I know within a second whether a joke is working or really shitting the bed. Writing a book, though, is another matter. I have nightmares about finishing it with a flare, getting hopeful, and selling eight copies. There's nothing worse than managers and agents who want to tell you the project you've worked so hard on sucks gorilla cock but can't, so they have to stand there and stammer on about how the economy is tanking and people just aren't buying books from mediocre, sex-addicted comedians at this time. And I am addicted to sex. As I write this I am waiting for a massage girl to come over. I'm getting the forty-minute special, which I imagine will end with me wiping tadpoles off my stomach.

I'm back. Not in some corny, "wait five seconds and pretend" way, either. The massage girl came over and thirty minutes into it began jerking me off. She was using both hands and looked like she was trying to yank a turnip out of the ground. I asked if she'd do anything else and she said occasionally she does oral but couldn't do it with me because she didn't have a condom. Fast-forward three minutes and a hundred dollars later, she's blowing me without a rubber. I know, I know, *"What about AIDS?"* Look, I don't want AIDS any more than the next fellow, but I suppose I'd rather catch it getting head from a cute twenty-four-year-old than stepping on a dirty needle in Seaside Heights. It wasn't a bad hummer, although I wish her stupid teeth wouldn't have spent so much time scraping my helmet. Don't women know when they're doing that? If I have a piece of broccoli stuck in my teeth it drives me nuts; how can you not tell when your molars are dragging over a spongey cockhead?

The upside of the blowjob was that it was rather wet and sloppy, which pleases me. I like to look down and see a girl drooling on my dick like a retard eating ice cream cake. For some reason I cannot finish this way with her, probably because in the back of my mind I am picturing Groucho Marx chomping down on a cigar as she clumsily bobs up and down. I finally pick up the lube and begin taking care of things myself and ask her to just lean over and lick my nipples, which she does with all the zeal of a kid going to the dentist (quite an accurate comparison, as during this encounter I have said things like, "Open up," "Spit," and "This will only hurt a little."). To get myself off I actually have to fantasize about another masseuse I see who gives better head. That should probably be an indication that you have a sexual problem: when you pay someone to blow you, and can't shoot your load unless you think about someone else you've paid to blow you. There really is something horribly lonely about that.

So back to lunch. We finished up and talked awhile over our cappuccinos (they were excellent, by the way, but the caffeine was so strong after four sips I had to excuse myself because I honestly thought I might shit my pants). I walked like I was on stilts because bending my legs would've loosened the clench of my ass cheeks just enough to send shit tumbling out all over the place. I came back to the table twenty minutes later and was embarrassed because she had to know I was shitting. I tried making up some excuse about how my contacts were bugging me and I had to keep taking them out, which I hoped would explain away the time I was gone. But we both knew I had been shitting. It was written all over my face.

I had never really considered writing a book. A written book is something I'd love to have, but the time and effort it takes to actually write one is my sticking point. When I think back, though, my very first laughs as a young kid came from stories I wrote. I would always write purposely funny things, then disingenuously act sheepish and shy and pretend I didn't want the teacher to read them. Believe me; I wanted them read. I'm sure had I been older, the thought, *I sure hope she reads my story*, would've morphed into, *Hurry up and get to it already, you cryptic meat bag.* Eventually, she'd read them and I'd always put on my horseshit "Aw, shucks, ma'am" routine, but inside I'd be beaming. I guess I still do that to a certain extent. I realize it's an irritating quality and I should knock it off already. Maybe the idea of not saying "I want this," somehow removes the risk in my mind? If I don't ask for it or show how much I want it, the inevitable failure will be less embarrassing and awful. It's the same thing when I like a girl. Instead of just walking up and saying something metrosexual like, "Hey, good looking, what's cooking?" I just look at her and imagine what a relationship with her might be like. How she and I would get to know each other, how we'd laugh, and what sex together might be like. Is she affectionate? Does she like her breasts kissed tenderly, or does she like them squeezed so hard she blacks out? It's usually at this point I realize I am staring at her and angrily masturbating.

One problem I've had when considering writing is that, other than prostitutes, I can't think of one subject I care about for two hundred pages. I get bored very quickly and things that seem fascinating to me today will make me want to slit my wrists a week later. This is why I have written in a pseudojournal form. It's just easier that way because I detest structure.

It's been three years since I wrote the preceding paragraphs. Not only is a book happening, but my deadline is in two weeks. Some of these writings are old writings; many were written specifically for this book. Who gives a shit, right? Hope you enjoy it.

HERE GOES NOTHING

WELL, THIS IS my first little entry. I am voluntarily writing a diary; I am now officially a fat girl. I don't know if I am doing this because it is somewhat cathartic or because I'm hoping to meet up with some incest survivor who will possibly perform oral sex on me. Don't misunderstand; I am not claiming to be too hip for the room right after knowingly walking into it, I am just not sure why I am doing it. I suppose there's a certain arrogance that goes with it. Every jackass who starts one of these does so with outwardly false humility, while inwardly thinking he's a true master who not only has important things to say, but whose wonderfulness will be discovered and gain him legions of devoted worshippers.

I am currently in Baltimore in my hotel room. Did three shows tonight and they went relatively well. It's frustrating to be down here because I don't draw worth a shit. In Philly and D.C. I do very well, but nobody in this awful, murderous shithole gives a good goddamn about my stupid act. The second show tonight had a decent-size crowd (which isn't saying much; second shows on Saturday *always* do well, in every club). The first and third shows were light, an accurate testament to the complete indifference Baltimore as a whole has for me. I did radio and television on Thursday morning and radio on Friday. All the press went well and still, fucking light shows. I feel like a complete dickhead standing outside in the lobby after each show whoring my CD and DVD.

Another irritation is that my throat is getting sore. I have been taking vitamin C and echinacea every day and the last time I got sick was in December, ironically the last time I was in Baltimore. It sucks being in a

11

city and drawing small crowds and not having an excuse. Back in December there were awful snowstorms, which secretly delighted me because I could speculate with the club owner how big the crowds would be if not for the snow. Well, no snow this week. Hopefully there's been some sort of SARS outbreak near the Inner Harbor that is keeping people inside. I hate being onstage and looking into the back of a half-empty room and seeing the waiters and waitresses sitting and watching the show. They're sitting because they have so few customers and watching because the only other option is to stand in the bathroom and stare at septic tanks. I know that they must hate me and see me as the reason they're making such shitty money that night. I actually feel bad. Not so much for them as for the smashing my ego is taking. An entire staff of servers wasting a Saturday night, not making any fucking money, and knowing *exactly* who to blame.

I can picture the hot waitress undressing in front of her boyfriend. "I hate when this fucking guy performs here; the shows are always empty blah blah blah. . . ." He probably consoles her with a great fuck while I jerk off once again like a zilch in my hotel bed. An out of shape, sweating, pear-shaped thirty-five-year-old dumping a load onto his belly while watching soft-core porn on SpectraVision. Enchanting. I so rarely get laid on the road, partially because I am too lazy to try and partially because I am such a far-gone pervert that if a girl doesn't just walk up to me and announce her intentions to use my face as a toilet, I have no interest.

I have one more show tomorrow night, Sunday, 7:00 p.m. Should be a real barn burner.

RUMPLESTILTSKIN

I OVERSLEPT BY *five* cocksucking hours today. I went to bed and called the operator to leave a 2:00 p.m. wake-up call. I also put a block on the phone because even with a DO NOT DISTURB sign on the door, some chimp from housekeeping will always call the room to ask if you need service. Nothing makes me want to perform a clitoral circumcision more than a stupid accent on the other end of the phone waking me up early. So I put the block on the phone *until my two p.m. wake-up call.* I then took a Melatonin pill to help me doze off. (Melatonin is a drug released by the brain to help you sleep. In pill form it affects me like shooting heroin or watching alternative comedy.)

I did wake up a few times throughout the course of the day, not realizing that I was oversleeping. At one point I had a very odd dream that I was using the urinal adjacent to one being used by Dick Van Dyke. He was pressed close to his but still managed to splatter me with piss. Very odd dream and I certainly hope it doesn't have the obvious homosexual implications it appears to have. How much therapy would it take for me to work through a deep-seated desire to be mouth-fucked and golden-showered by Rob Petrie? Hopefully it represents something entirely benign, like my mind waking me up to urinate, or maybe I just want to teabag Mary Tyler Moore.

Sexy Dick Van Dyke dream aside, the next thing I am conscious of is a knocking at my door. It's the bellman, telling me I have a ride waiting downstairs. I look at the clock and it is 7:01 p.m. (showtime is at seven), so I panic and throw on clothes, rinse my mouth out with toothpaste, and run out of the room disheveled with my balls smelling like a Muenster and onion sandwich. In the truck I am trying to casually explain why I am waking up that late, and I know the owner is thinking I am a drug addict, a drunk, or just a total ass. The show went well except for the fact that the entire time I was performing I had to take a dump the size of Shaq's forearm.

A guy who I met in January at the porn awards showed up. Every year in Vegas, there is a three-day porn expo that leads up to the AVN Awards on Saturday night. I was hosting with Jenna Jameson later that evening. I was hanging out during the day in Evil Angel's signing booth when Mike Tyson walked in. There's a cool video of Tyson with his arm around me, making me promise to refer to him as a pimp at the awards show. In this pic it looks as if someone shouted out, "Hey, Mike, whose ass are you going to fuck?" and Mike is responding, "His."

I came back to the room tonight, packed, ate a hamburger, and drove back to New York right after. Because I packed and ate after the show instead of before, I missed getting back in time to watch a porn shoot my friend was involved in. I hope the hotel operator who made the error one day oversleeps as a five-alarm fire is ravaging her house. As soon as I arrived home I ordered an escort named Kathy; very juicy, full lips, and a nice hiney. As soon as we finished I began to suspect she was a postop transsexual. I don't know why I felt that way; she had no Adam's apple or anything, just a gut feeling. I watched her pee and she kind of covered her pussy a bit while she did it, which made me think she was pointing something downward. Who knows and who gives a hoot. It's not gay once surgery is involved, wink wink, nudge nudge. It's a little after 4:00 a.m. and I am about to order a club sandwich. No wonder I'm a fat-titted nothing.

THE MASSAGE

I ENJOY GETTING massages occasionally to alleviate the stress in my shoulders, as well as the stress in my balls. One of my semiregulars came over; we do half-hour sessions, which is great. There's nothing worse during a massage than tolerating all of the shoulder rubbing while patiently waiting for a finger to mosey on down to your anus. When you have a thirty-minute session, there is none of that "attempt to look legitimate" silliness.

In preparation for my massage, I lay towels on my bed (due to the oil she will use; I don't want it staining my sheets. Logs are okay on the chest but don't get oil on my bed. A slight inconsistency in thinking.). She comes over and strips down to her bra and panties. She is in her early forties, slim with dirty blond hair. But she's not slim in the classic, sexy, slim kind of way. She has a body that would look good getting out of a tub in *The Shining*. But she has great hands, so I lay on my stomach to begin.

She started off by kneeling at my side, using her hands in sweeping strokes over my back and lightly on my ass. She kept leaning over so her breasts rubbed against me while her arms went in either direction. It was quite a nice feeling and whenever her hand brushed over my dumper I gave the subtle, sexy signal of pumping my hips up and down. I looked like a dog scratching my vaginal lips on a carpet. Her light touches on my ass were really making me happy; and when a finger happened to slip in a bit, I felt it would be rude to say anything. Technically she was a guest in my home, and if she wanted to insert a slippery finger into my asshole, who was I to be a curmudgeon about it?

Now that I had oil on my back and a digit in my crack, it was time to turn over for the main event. This enchanting gal immediately began grabbing my mule and talking to me in her German/Austrian accent. It was sexy, yet I was also waiting for her to start peeking in my mouth for gold teeth. I begin playing with her breasts, but she wouldn't move her arm for me to give the nipple a neighborly kiss. Of course I wanted to lower her panties for a vaginal peek, which she wasn't happy about either. I was rubbing her hiney while she fingered mine and tugged my penis and talked to me sounding not unlike Arnold Schwarzenegger. She was getting irritated with my groping (apparently what's good for the goose is *not* good for the gander) and told me to stop, that she'd been generous enough. I stopped, and suddenly felt like a boy who'd been caught with his hand in the cookie jar (or in this case, the boy who'd been caught with his finger in the Nazi). I was trying to keep my mood but invariably, my dick wilted like scalding tea was spilled on my bag. And instead of just keeping going, this idiot told me that we only had four minutes left. *Four minutes?* How exact a fucking number is that? Rotten fucking Hun. I just stopped her and said forget it. I stood up and got dressed, which was her hint to leave. It really was a very Don Corleone–like dismissal. She apologized as she was getting dressed (she probably figured I'd freak or be abusive or ask for the money back, which I didn't) and that was that. So she left with my money while I sat there with a bag full of needing-to-be-released seeds. I jerked off like a lab animal and then went to sleep. I showed her.

MORBID OBESITY

I WAS WATCHING a special earlier tonight on Discovery Health Channel about a woman named Kathy who was having stomach-stapling surgery. Kathy wouldn't have been bad looking if she dropped two hundred pounds and stopped wearing her hair like the Hulk. She actually looked a lot like Augustus Gloop. The documentary narrator must have said the words "morbidly obese" about forty times. I loved it. I don't know why, but I enjoy those words very much. Maybe because they're so brutally honest. So, how was your blind date? "Morbidly obese." Not a lot of room for interpretation there. It's probably not a term used very often in singles ads. *"Morbidly obese woman seeks morbidly obese gentleman for friendship and geometrically impossible attempts at intercourse. Must enjoy strenuous activities such as breathing, shoe tying, and taking long, romantic walks to the kitchen. I love dogs and horses as well as traditional luncheon meats. My favorite films are* Shallow Hal *and anything starring Marlon Brando after 1980. You must be sincere, intelligent, and adept at barnacle removal."*

I sure would hate to be stricken with morbid obesity. I wonder how the doctor words that to a patient. *"Well, Kathy, as everyone in the free world already knows, you're obese. Now I hate to be the bearer of such news, but I'm sure your suspicions were already aroused by things like creaking floorboards and housedresses that were mistaken for car covers. I feel it's my duty to inform you that your obesity has shot past unpleasant, sailed right over disgusting, made a brief stop at horrendous, and finally landed on morbid."*

This portly enchantress (no, this is not Kathy) rode me like a pony in front of almost three thousand people the night I hosted Babefest for WYSP in Philly.

As I watched this special I started to feel bad for Kathy. Sure, at first I was yelling, "Die, Fatso!" and throwing butter cookies at the screen; it's only natural. Initially she weighed about four hundred pounds and was quite miserable. They showed some great footage of her wheezing to the mailbox and talking to her husband. He was a svelte little thing and looked like Billy Bob Thornton, with a stupid smile plastered on his face the whole time. I never quite understood skinny guys who like fatties. They're called "chubby chasers" and I suspect it has to do with a fear of being abandoned. (Four-hundred-pound women don't just up and leave you because (a) no one else will fuck them, and (b) getting up and leaving would waste precious energy that could be better spent raiding the refrigerator like a Viking.) Either that, or maybe these guys just love being hugged by those giant, awful arms so they can feel safe and secure like mommy made them feel. Or perhaps it's something simple, like enjoying massive tits that smell like a potpie when you lick underneath them.

Either way, during the interviews Kathy was saying that she wanted to drop 260 pounds to get down to 140. I admired the fact she wanted to lose all of it and not just get down to water-buffalo weight. She had this tiny white negligee that she used as a motivator. She put it over her fat head before the surgery and it just hung around her neck like an apron. Her goal was to lose enough tonnage to wear it for her husband. He seemed like a nice chap, and said that as far as her surgery was concerned, it didn't matter to him as long as she was happy. He's a better man than me. I would have long ago presented her with an ultimatum: Either go through with the surgery and get down to a decent size, or I'm going to start fucking the children.

Six months after the surgery she'd lost something like 110 pounds and I was pleased for her. I am grateful I am not in her shoes (although I'm sure they'd be much happier shoes if I were; *RIMSHOT!*) Truth be told, I do empathize with her. I certainly understand unhealthy addiction. For me, it's porn and hookers; for years it was drugs and alcohol, and until a couple of years ago, cigarettes as well. I love anything that removes me from the present. And I do eat compulsively, but so far it hasn't done more than add fifteen extra pounds, which I'd lose if I didn't have the exercise regimen of a truncated burn victim.

I think I liked Kathy because she wasn't a typically melodramatic, crying fat girl on camera. No hand-holding malarkey, no attempts at yanking emotion out of the viewer. As she was being wheeled into surgery on a gurney (which was quite a visual. It reminded me of the government transporting a ballistic missile all covered up on the back of a flatbed truck), she admitted she was frightened but had faith in God, and then mercifully, they administered drugs and sent this sea cow off to la-la land.

The special ended with her at about 240 pounds or so, but by this time she may have lost a lot more. Either that or she just kept eating until she ended up as a scene from *The Meaning of Life*. I am optimistic for her, though; she seemed very committed. At one point they showed her and a couple of hundred other plus-sized delights volunteering to go on a march to raise obesity awareness. A march is probably not necessary, as you become aware of obesity when you're stuck next to one of these manatees on a cross-country flight or one of them steps on your foot. I hope they try

21

that march here in New York and city officials make them walk through the Midtown tunnel like a herd of circus elephants.

Kathy was doing well and I hope she made it. I hope she hit her goal weight and finally got to put on that little negligee for her husband after a candlelit salad for two. I can picture her seductively sauntering into the bedroom wearing it, then him not being able to get an erection. She'll ask what's wrong and he'll break down crying and admit he's gay. This will send her spiraling into a depression and she'll seek solace by filling her tennis ball–size stomach with a Velamint and two garbanzo beans. In a last-ditch effort to seduce him she'll put on the outfit she was wearing the day they met: a leopard-print dress made from the living-room curtains of a Puerto Rican. When this doesn't work, she'll perform oral sex on him. His limp, noodley dick will subconsciously remind her of lo mein, which will cause her to pour duck sauce on it and eat it.

If it weren't for shit, prostitutes, and fat girls, this book would be about eight pages long. I'm a three-trick pony and an ass. See you later, alligators.

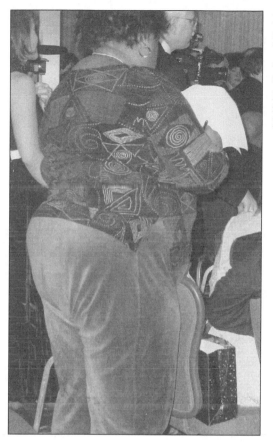

I took this photo last year; it is simply the worst ass on earth. This woman is black and obese and *still* managed to have a flat, awful pancake ass. I only photographed her because at first glance I thought she was Patrice Oneal.

LAS VEGAS

TRAVELING ALWAYS MAKES me tired and lazy. I got to Vegas on Friday morning and spent the early part of the day in the Sprint store with Bob Kelly. I had just come off a plane, it was over a hundred degrees out, and my asshole itched like there was a small ant colony break dancing in it. I was in no mood to deal with some faggoty salesman and was honestly afraid I would throw my nonworking phone right at his teeth. I didn't have to worry, though; the guy who helped me actually upgraded me to a better phone free of charge, so my anger drained away quickly. We stood outside for an hour waiting for the hotel van to come and get us, and I was seriously debating hitchhiking. Of course, I was aware of all the possible dangers of hitchhiking, but I didn't figure we were particularly good rape candidates. And to be honest, I wouldn't have cared if someone plugged my asshole with dynamite if it did anything to ease the *incessant* itching.

My first day was a fun hang, but I didn't really do too much. Me and stupid Bob just hung around the casino looking at box and losing money. We shoved a lot of food into our fat faces as well. And if you're in Vegas and you want to look at girls, the Hard Rock is without a doubt where you want to be. I've never been tempted to actually jack off on a casino floor (which is probably legal in Vegas as long as you're gambling while you do it).

I slept really late on Saturday and woke up frustrated and cranky. I refused to go anywhere near the pool; my self-esteem couldn't handle it. We went to a show rehearsal around six for *Beacher's Comedy Madhouse*, which is run by a guy named Jeff Beacher. He's an interesting character and a great promoter, but he looks like Jake LaMotta in the second half of *Raging Bull*. This show is unlike any other I've done; it's got dancers and music and a talent show, as well as a six-foot-eight bisexual Russian sword swallower. After talking to him for thirty seconds I understood why he had no gag reflex. He finished the show by prancing around in a pink fur with a big pink feather hat. He couldn't have looked more feminine if he had been breast-feeding in a Markie Post movie on the Oxygen network.

There are a shitload of hot chicks in the show, none of whom would even look at me. It is a *very* rowdy crowd and there's at least an hour of music and dancing before comics are on. Bob Kelly went up and had a great show. I really was rooting for him to take a nice bombing on the chin so I would look better.

After Bob there was a brief freak parade onstage and then I was announced. I did well but not great; Bob definitely did better. (That could be the hardest sentence I've ever had to write; the only thing I ever want Bob to do better is die in a fiery boating accident.) I was slightly depressed after the show so we went to the new club in the Hard Rock basement. The casino owner is a young guy named Harry Morton, who took great care of us, VIP seating in the club with free beverages. No pussy for me, of course. At the end of the night I was walking back to the room and I saw Chuck Zito at a poker machine. He's a very large Hell's Angel who was also a cast member of *Oz*. He is most famous for knocking out Jean Claude Van Damme at Scores strip club in New York City. I asked him for a photo and he was surprisingly pleasant. (Yes, I did just use the words "surprisingly pleasant" to describe Chuck Zito. I don't know why, but in the presence of real men, I turn into a fucking Jewish grandmother.)

I wound up staying in Vegas the next day. I never take time to do shit like that and it was well worth it. On Sunday afternoon around five, a smoking twenty-year-old prostitute came to my room, courtesy of Jeff

Beacher. She drank from my mule and made me very happy. I then went down and met Bob and some friends in the diner, and Chuck Zito popped in and ate with us. Me and that fat idiot Bob were asking him tough-guy questions like a couple of swooning fairies: "Mr. Zito, did you ever punch someone really hard??" and, "Were the people in prison scary, Mr. Zito??" We both traipsed to the gift shop in our high heels to buy copies of his book so he'd sign them for us.

A mercifully blurry photo of me and Chuck.

I was completely disgusted with my lack of manliness. I enjoyed eating with him but the more he talked about kicking asses the more I felt like a crossdressing slug. I went upstairs and saw another prostitute. One of the finest ever. Kissing, tinkling, and fucking. What a terrific gal.

SITCOMS

DUE TO THE horrendously unfunny nature of most television sitcoms, I've decided to get involved in the process. Many of my ideas are quite progressive, if I may be permitted to toot my own horn. Conceptually, I cannot decide which one I love the most, so I will probably try to find a way to pitch them all.

The first is a touching, hour-long weekly comedy/drama about three women over four hundred pounds each who battle their weight and low self-esteem. The working title is *Treadmill, You Spectacle*. I want it set somewhere in the Midwest so that each week a different one of them can have a leg or hip shattered in a case of mistaken identity during a cow tipping. I'd also like to see different male stars make cameos throughout the season playing various love interests. I have a fabulous script already written where one of the girls meets a handsome doctor and falls in love. He sweeps her off her feet using plagiarized poetry and a bulldozer, so she agrees to marry him and fly to Havana for their honeymoon. Before they board the plane he forces her to shove thirty powder-filled balloons into her anus. While they are collecting their luggage at baggage claim, drug-sniffing German shepherds begin barking and snapping at her asshole. Her husband begins pointing at her and screaming, "Heroin mule, heroin mule!" as she is tackled and beaten into unconsciousness by Cuban customs agents.

She is thrown into a five-foot-by-seven-foot cell where she develops cervical cancer and dies awaiting trial. Her husband actually turns out to be a professional prankster who specializes in setting obese women up to be beaten and jailed in Third World countries. Either Harvey Keitel or Keanu

Reeves should be cast in the part of the scoundrel. I am anticipating far more trouble casting the wife because the only two actresses I will accept are both dead.

I also have an idea for a show that would revolve around a mediocre man with supple tits and lower-back fat who picks up transgendered friends for oral treats. He pays these friends in Euros and pretends not to notice their Adam's apples. He has no girlfriend and his hobbies are making up racist flyers and covering his head with the bedsheets to better enjoy his own chronic foot odor and cabbage farts. He is also something of a special agent, although instead of solving international crimes he uses all of his wares and influences to help friends exploit loopholes in Megan's Law. The name of the show will be either *My Life* or *Adventures of a Tongue Sniffer*. I am not completely sure if I will have siblings for this character or just a wacky neighbor who always comes over wearing an EAT MY ASSHOLE T-shirt. Some of the script may be slightly racy for softer-than-normal network television, but I will absolutely not compromise on the dialogue; good shows live and die with likeable characters and believable interaction.

One scene I can already foresee being a problem is when the main character (whose name is Francis Cunte) goes to the shop to pick up his car, which he has damaged while committing a vehicular homicide during an alcoholic blackout. When he shows up for his car, the mean-spirited mechanic informs Francis that Allstate does *not* cover having blood, hair ribbons, and a teddy bear removed from his front grill. Francis is livid; he only has eight dollars in cash and $200,000 in Monopoly money in the trunk. The mechanic (I am hoping to land Edward James Olmos to play this semirecurring role) tells Francis to take a long walk off a short pier and Francis responds by knocking out all of his upper teeth with a wrench (his own teeth, not the mechanic's). The police are called and Francis is charged with drunk driving, second-degree murder, and being a silly goose. This will be not only the season premiere but a two-part episode. I originally wrote it so that he got the death penalty, but I thought death would be detrimental for character development. So I decided that in part two he will be acquitted on the technicality that he is white and pure.

I've also had an obsessive interest with writing a sitcom around a dog of some sort, perhaps an Irish setter, maybe even a bull mastiff. The premise would be that he's a drug-sniffing dog who can never do his job properly due to sinus allergies. He tries everything, and in the process becomes addicted to Afrin. He's eventually fired by the sheriff's department due to an unrelated homosexual incident. Weeks later, he is found by his bitch, hanging in the closet with his pants around his ankles and a Breathe Right strip on his nose.

A ROAD STORY

YEARS AGO, I did a weekend gig with Jim Florentine in North Carolina. I honestly can't remember anything about the gig itself other than it was awful. Just one of the many no-name, no-longer-featuring-comedy shit houses I did when building what would eventually become my foundation as a stand-up. Back in those days there were a lot of Friday/Saturday hotel gigs; the big boom of the eighties was over, but there were still plenty of places willing to give comics terrible money to humiliate themselves on parquet dance floors in one-star hotel conference rooms. I started in 1990, so I mention the eighties boom by reputation only. The majority of one-nighters had dried up by the time I showed up, so in my first few years I was constantly assaulted with stories about pockets full of cash and waitresses lining up to suck the headliner's dick. (Many of these stories were told by horribly unfunny men wearing awful blazers, jeans, and pencil-thin "I'm a comedian" ties. Mercifully, most of them have been systematically drummed out of the business.)

Stories about road pussy always fascinated me, though. The concept of being paid for being funny was amazing enough; the idea that women would fuck you for it was almost incomprehensible. I was probably doing comedy for a year before I got even remotely close to a taste of comedy-groupie puss. It was a midweek one-nighter in Connecticut, headlined by Bob Levy and middled by Jim. I was the MC (meaning I went up first and attempted to warm up the crowd) and had very little road experience, yet somehow wound up pulling off a decent set. In my first couple of years as a stand-up I was a high-energy, desperate-for-approval shithead. I oversold jokes, made muggy faces, and in true jizzbucket fashion, wore baggy MC Hammer pants. I've seen many photos of myself from those days, standing there in those horrid pants. I literally swam in them, which from the waist down made me look like the Grimace with AIDS.

My first headshot, around 1990. A true ass trying to strike a funny pose. Notice not only the revolting pants, but the dark pit stains and fashionable shoes.

After the show we were sitting at a long table with some locals who were reveling in the comic aura of the three Jersey dumbbells who had just entertained them. I was sitting next to a girl who was there with some guys. She started rubbing my leg under the table and making eye contact with me and I honestly thought I was going to blow a load in my pants. I could *not believe* this was happening. The fact that she looked like Rocky Dennis was irrelevant; she was willing to fuck *me* because I was funny. I managed to convince this Down's syndrome–headed drunkard to walk me to the car under the guise of signing a headshot for her. I desperately wanted to sit her in the passenger seat and shove my dick into her mouth like a pacifier. Unfortunately, her friends were cockblockers and all stood in the doorway and watched us the entire time. There immediately followed the awkward moment of me fake-looking for headshots I knew weren't there before we both walked away disappointed; me with blue balls and the Elephant Man with a barely legible autograph scribbled on a wet bar napkin.

I sat in the backseat, miserable, for the ride home. Since it was his car, Jim drove and Levy was in the passenger seat (Bob never drove to gigs due to his acute alcoholism). It was dark and I was as sexually frustrated as I've ever been, so I decided to quietly unzip my purple pants and jerk off (that should produce a beehive of putrid mental images). Quietly masturbating in the back of a dark vehicle while your buddies carry on and laugh up front is not only disgustingly creepy, it's more than slightly homoerotic. Doing this while wearing baggy purple pants should be punishable by death. Anyway, something in my quiet backseat demeanor tipped off Jim and he turned on the interior light, catching me. He gave me something of a scolding and I reluctantly put my penis away. I wasn't as embarrassed at getting caught as much as I was irritated that I couldn't finish.

This particular story is not about the Connecticut highway incident. Nor is it about the Maryland hotel incident, when Bob and I wacked off onto the television screen just to give Jim something unpleasant to look at when he came back from fucking whichever waitress he'd picked up. Like two eager beavers we waited for him to come back and discover our mischief. Upon entering the room, Jim saw the two loads on the TV, mumbled, "Beautiful," then promptly went to bed.

This particular story is about North Carolina, and it occurred years later. Jim and I had done some gig where I think we performed on a dance floor with a mic stand on it. We finished the Saturday show and planned on leaving for home immediately. It's always easier to drive at night and avoid traffic; there's nothing worse than trying to sleep while your head keeps telling you how much closer to home you could be if you were in the car already. Our shit was all packed in the trunk and ready for travel.

Before the show we agreed that we'd stick around if anyone in possession of a vagina was willing to speak to us. Of course right after the show a sexy little Southern girl approaches Jim. She not only had a fat friend with her, she had the *quintessential* fat friend: unpleasant, sulking, and complaining that she wanted to leave. I empathized with her, I wanted to hightail it out of there as well, but as male rules dictate, if Jim has a shot at emptying his ballbag on someone, I am obligated to be a team player and wait it out. No questions asked, I began to occupy the kvetching fatso and feign interest in whatever it was she was yapping about. Jim was practically sodomizing Mary Lou Retton at the table while I engaged in a PETA discussion with Gilbert Grapes's mother. At one point Jim and the girl got up to go to the bar and ended up being gone about twenty minutes. I knew what was going on and had to keep this fat fuck occupied because every two minutes she was wondering aloud about the whereabouts of her friend. I really detest passive-aggressive shit like this; she knew they were probably fooling around and yet this jealous slob wanted to ruin it under the guise of being concerned.

Finally, they returned and Jim had the relaxed swagger of one who has just been relieved of semen (she blew him in the bathroom). We figured we'd stay a few minutes to engage in the obligatory afterload chitchat so she didn't call local police and file rape charges just to teach him a lesson in manners. While we were talking one of her other friends showed up, this one a very attractive girl. I was just happy to have a chick at the table under four hundred pounds who wasn't picking splooge out of her teeth. As it normally is with hot girls, she wanted *nothing* to do with me. She not only wouldn't talk to me, she wouldn't look at me. I think the whole PETA/ animal rights thing came up again and I must have babbled out the correct words because all of a sudden she was interested in what I had to say. From zero to sixty in about ten seconds, she and I were suddenly chatting up a storm. Of course the toxic elephant was trying to interject, but being the true blue individual he is, Jim jumped in and began to run blocker on the fatty for me. Even Ole Cum Gullet got the hint and helped Jim distract her awful friend while Sexy New Friend and I hit it off. We somehow decided to go back to the room and unceremoniously blow off the awful fatty. She tried one of the "Fine, I'm going home" routines that has been mastered by the American Fat Girl, but to their credit, both girls pretty much told her to drive safe.

We all headed to Jim's room to talk and hopefully get me some sort of sexual activity. We brought alcohol for the girls and some coffee and pretzels for me (coffee breath and matted pretzel in your teeth should always be a prerequisite for making out). Jim and Girl #1 started in immediately on the other bed kissing and grinding while Hot Friend and I tried to talk maturely and pretend *Behind the Green Door* wasn't being shot two feet to our left. I finally made a move and to my surprise she went with it. By this time, Florentine and the chick were naked while we were still in the "kiss your neck and brush a little hair away from your face" stage. Seeing them nude was depressing because Jim's in much better shape than I am; so now I couldn't take my shirt off because my unsightly man-tits would jiggle all over the place.

They were in the next bed, now fucking, and Hot But Getting Bored Friend and I were fully clothed. I finally got her skirt up and proceeded to go down on her and she kept trying to get my clothes off so we could bang. There was *no way* I was going to be able to perform sexually with all that pressure, especially with Jim and his date fucking like champs and glancing over to see what was going on with us. I was the only loser in the room fully clothed (I was wearing black from head to toe) and finally took my dick out so she could go down on me and attempt to get me hard, so I could give her what would undoubtedly be remembered as the worst fuck of her life. She was performing oral treats on me (and well, I might add), but because I was nervous my cock was shriveled up like a mealworm. I knew this was a lost cause so I awkwardly laid her back and began going down on her again; a true admission of defeat.

I literally ate her for two hours and she kept getting close and then pushing my head away because she was afraid to let go and orgasm. Lovely. Not only can I publicly not get an erection, but she has to work through preteen molestation issues while they pound away loudly next to us. The whole time Jim's girl was screaming and he was grunting, "Hrrrrmmmph, hrrrrrmph, grrrrrr," while I laid between my date's legs and made slurping sounds similar to those a cancer patient makes while eating hospital broth with a spork. Nothing worse on Earth than watching your naked, in-shape friend *pound* a pussy while you lay with a limp dick, dressed like the preacher from *Poltergeist 2*. Mercifully, they finally stopped so the only sounds left in the room were my lips smacking and her muffled attempts to keep repressed memories from flying out and ruining all of our good fun.

I don't remember what finally stopped our equally dysfunctional humiliation marathon. She may have started text messaging with her grandmother, or perhaps I got the hint when her clit piped up and asked for Chapstick. Either way, we slept for about two hours then headed back to New Jersey. Jim and his girl kept in touch for a year, having phone sex, and, not surprisingly, my calls went unreturned. Too bad she didn't live in Connecticut; she could have just sat in the car with Jim and Bob and watched me jerk off in the backseat.

I'M A POET AND DIDN'T KNOW IT

AS MANY OF you know, I went to rehab in January 1986 after a halfhearted, insincere suicide attempt. It was a place called the Princeton House in New Jersey. The people and counselors there were genuinely nice and I did learn things while I was there. Not enough, though, as my roommate, Dwayne, and I drank one night in our rooms; he had a pint of wine, I had a half pint of vodka. Our friend Harvey, who used to get drunk and follow police cars, drank a few beers that night as well. I think I blabbed to someone in the rehab thinking I was hot shit. (When I was just a small boy my friend would always say, "You think you're hot shit on a silver platter but you're really just cold piss on a paper plate." He was quite the wordsmith. If he dies tomorrow it won't be soon enough.) Anyway, I bragged to another patient and they told one of the counselors. Everyone had to have a big meeting and the counselor confronted us. Dwayne and Harvey admitted it and got booted out; I lied through my seventeen-year-old teeth so I wouldn't get sent to a long-term treatment facility. Michael Corleone would have been proud. I said, "No, I didn't drink," and everyone knew I was fucking lying.

My first week there (it was a thirty-day program. The drinking incident happened about a week before I was scheduled to leave), I wrote this cheesy, horrendous-attempt-at-heartstring-tug of a poem. I couldn't wait for everyone to read it. But I couldn't just start handing it out; that would be too obviously desperate and transparently needy. So I did what any complete boob would do: I anonymously left it on someone's bed. I can understand if reading that makes you want to brain me because as I am relating this story, I'm having a strong desire to mash my own newtish face into the computer monitor. Do you understand? *I left it on someone's bed.* You know, so they'd find it and the big mystery would begin. It actually worked like a charm. All of these dumbbells are passing around this *drivel* and wondering who had left such a gift. Who is this shy, passionate genius? I bumbled around the rehab trying to start conversations about it, watching out of the corner of my eye as people read it. Finally, someone asked me and I confessed. It wasn't quite the moment I'd hoped for (and it certainly wasn't the moment I deserved; if it was, a fucking anvil would have fallen out of the ceiling onto my head). Everyone was pretty much over it by the time Jimmy Allen Poe claimed his treasure while beaming with pride. Once in group I even tried to slip it in while I was talking, " . . . and I wrote this poem that people seem to like . . ." and to their credit they reacted appropriately: with total indifference. I think that by that point, even though all of them were mental cases not even a month clean, they saw what an unabridged idiot I was.

I am really glad I dug this up, but reading it gave me the kind of feeling you get when you remember the alcohol breath of the family friend who came into your room to "tuck you in" an hour after everyone went to bed. This would be bad enough if I wrote it when I was eleven, but I was seven months away from legally voting and being eligible for the death penalty. Here are photos of this masterpiece so you can get a taste of my handsome writing style. I have also transcribed it, in its entirety, for your reading pleasure. Please take note of the classic rhyming scheme I don't attempt to deviate from even for a second. Enjoy it at your leisure; hankies and tissues are optional.

'ODE TO SOME OLD FRIENDS'

Here I lay in princeton House just staring at
the ceiling
Between these walls they've taught me how to
deal with all my feelings
I hid my pain down deep inside, I tucked it all
away
The pain it grew, it ate at me, it killed me day
by day

I had a friend, he helped me cope, named Johnnie
Walker Red
It hurt inside to learn the truth, he'd rather
see me dead
Jack Daniels was another one, a so-called friend
of mine
I'd wrap my lips around his neck, he'd leave
me feeling fine
Jack Daniels too, had lied to me, I'd been
decieved again
So I set out in desperate hope to find a
loyal friend
Depressed no more, my spirits soared, I was no
longer sad
For I soon met a Southerner by the name of

41

Old Granddad
Held lead me to the promised land, the road
we'd start to pave
But the only road this bastard knew was a
short cut to the grave
I left these friends not knowing that my end was
drawing near
Quite sheep thought I, to leave the rye, the
gin and everclear
I'd be o.k. If every day I'd stick to only
beer
But I'd been tricked and my disease would
look at me and sneer
But this "social drink" made glamorous by
commercials on T.V.
Would take its toll, I'd sell my soul, it was
my enemy
I knew not why I couldn't find a friend
who'd really help
But then I knew the time was here, it was time
to help myself
My mind wassick, my body scarred, my life
was at its low
But light shined through, the Princeton House,
like a fire in the snow

I'm happy now, my life is good &
hope is shiny m

But the worst part of this mood
however is that to suicide means town

The original poem. F for content, A for penmanship.

ODE TO SOME OLD FRIENDS

Here I lay at Princeton House just staring at the ceiling

I suppose the first question would have to be: If I am staring at the ceiling, how am I writing? Am I on my back, holding the notebook out in front of my face like Michelangelo? Or maybe I wasn't staring at the ceiling at all; maybe I was on the toilet but couldn't get it to rhyme with the next line. Either way, the opening sentence reeks of teenage melodrama.

Between these walls they've taught me how to deal with all my feelings

They actually taught me nothing of the sort. They taught me how to jerk off in my room thinking about a redheaded fellow inpatient named Jennifer.

I hid my pain down deep inside, I tucked it all away

Apparently I thought slicing my wrists and calling the FBI at 3:00 a.m. were exercises in subtlety. Not only did I not keep pain inside or tucked away, but I wore it on my sleeve and irritated people until they acknowledged it.

The pain it grew, it ate at me, it killed me day by day

It is after this line I'd like the dramatic organ music to start, please.

I had a friend, he helped me cope, named Johnnie Walker Red
It hurt inside to learn the truth, he'd rather see me dead

I've since learned from sources that Johnnie wanted me dead, but only once he'd read my poetry.

Jack Daniel's was another one, a so-called friend of mine

In hindsight, I realize what a lucky coincidence it was that I only drank things named after people. This poem would have seemed silly if I had to write things like, "Meister Brau was another one . . ." or, "Michelob wanted me dead after he and peach Schnapps talked it over and concurred that I was an ass . . ."

I'd wrap my lips around his neck, he'd leave me feeling fine

Too bad I didn't wrap my lips around a shotgun barrel; I could have prevented this embarrassment for all of us.

Jack Daniel's, too, had lied to me, I'd been deceived again
So I set out in desperate hope to find a loyal friend

If I'd have known then what I know now about peanut butter and where you can put it to have a dog lick it off, finding a loyal friend would have been a piece of cake.

Happy Endings

Depressed no more, my spirits soared, I was no longer sad
For I soon met a Southerner by the name of Old Granddad

A major problem with teenage angst poetry is that you begin to write in what is not your natural voice or cadence just to get the rhyme for the next line set up. "My spirits soared"? I was a no-impact, nothing of a suburban idiot, why are my spirits suddenly soaring? Not to mention that Old Granddad is a gasoline-like whiskey that made me sick every time I drank it.

He'd lead me to the promised land, the road we'd start to pave
But the only road this bastard knew was a shortcut to the grave

That's right, folks; pardon my French but he was a bastard! And I know a lot of you are thinking that I brought this on myself; I mean if Johnnie and Jack were such tricksters, why should Granddad be any different? But it really could've happened to anyone. We were paving, it was hot, he said he knew a shortcut. You know how it goes.

I left these friends not knowing that my end was drawing near
Quite sheep, thought I, to leave the rye, the gin and everclear

As I read this line I almost got physically ill. "Quite sheep, thought I"? I suppose it's normal for most seventeen-year-olds to go through a brief "British aristocrat" phase halfway through a drippy poem. Not only is this line horrid on every level, but I stole it from A Clockwork Orange. *Malcolm McDowell did not, however, take the time to rhyme it with anything, which is why you don't want to smash him in the mouth when he says it.*

I'd be o.k. if every day I'd stick to only beer
But I'd been tricked and my disease would look at me and sneer

As it should have. My disease must have realized it was dealing with an almost adult who had the idea-conveying ability of a six-year-old. Sneering was probably the only recourse it had to avoid vomiting while I pontificated about pain and things of that ilk.

But this "social drink" made glamorous by commercials on TV
Would take its toll, I'd sell my soul, it was my enemy

Instead of my soul, I should have sold my poetry and used the proceeds to buy cyanide.

I knew not why I couldn't find a friend who'd really help

"I knew not why . . ." Once again, without provocation, I am speaking like King Lear.

But then I knew the time was here, it was time to help myself

Unfortunately, I didn't help myself to any college courses or a thesaurus.

My mind was sick, my body scarred, my life was at its low
But light shined through, the Princeton House, like a fire in the snow

And lucky for me that in snow, fire stands out rather nicely. It made the Princeton House much easier to find. Had it stood out like a fire in a volcano,

I'd probably still be wandering around like a complete idiot and spouting sentiments that belong at the end of a Molly Ringwald movie.

I'm happy now, my life is good & hope is shining in

I wasn't, it wasn't, and it wasn't.

But the worst part of this mad disease is that to surrender means to win

That's right, ladies and gentlemen, it's a mad disease—mad, I tell you! And incidentally, not to correct my learned teenage self, but the worst part of alcoholism isn't that "surrendering is winning"; that's actually the best part. The worst part would have to be the lack of judgment one gets when attempting to be poignant and introspective. You think you're really hitting emotional home runs when in fact you're coming off sounding like Dr. Seuss after listening to his first Nirvana album.

The last thing I'd like to point out is the audacity of naming this "Ode to Some Old Friends." I lived in North Brunswick, which is a small, whitebread town in central New Jersey. And I lived with my parents; the fucking nerve of me to try and come off like a rustic old cattle hand. An ode is a lyrical poem of some length and is supposed to be contemplative in nature. More accurate names would have been "Rhymes That Could Just As Easily Have Been Written by a Retarded Child," or, "If You Well Up Reading This, You'll Be Shot."

Well, I hope you enjoyed our little sashay down memory lane. That brings us to the conclusion of this week's episode of *A Douche Bag: The Early Years.*

PINK EYE

I WOKE UP yesterday at 4:15 p.m., which is perfect because I had a 4:45 call time for *Tough Crowd*. Nothing like a cool half hour to work out those cobwebs and prepare for a television show. I showered and ran out the door, feeling like a lazy shitbag as I caught a cab to go ten blocks.

No one wanted to stand within twenty feet of me due to the fact that my stupid right eye was pinkish and bloodshot. People act like pink eye is the fucking bubonic plague. I wanted to pick out my eye gunk and put it on someone's lip gloss. I needed medication but everything in this stupid country is prescription, which means I'd have to go to a doctor and that takes time. I bought some medication that's supposed to be fairly good and put a few drops in my eye. It was rather refreshing if you like battery acid on your pupils. I vaguely remember a woman I know (who happens to have fat, juicy vaginal lips; *nice*) once told me that squeezing a lemon into your eye kills pink eye. If I remember correctly she was a sadist and a psychopath and probably just told me that so if I ever got it I'd needlessly put myself through agony.

So anyway, I did *Tough Crowd* and really stunk up the joint. I was witless and awful yesterday, sitting there most of the time with an amused, half-retarded look on my face. I got to the Comedy Cellar for my 1:00 a.m. spot and find out that NBC has been taping all night. The first time a major network is taping there and I am on at one in the morning with a yeast infection in my eye. I told them I wouldn't sign a release so they didn't film me.

I am tired of goddamn comedy documentaries anyway. They never show it like it is, just a few melodramatic jerkoff comics trying to look tortured while saying, "Comedy is all I know, man . . ." And reporters always feel the need to interject their idiotic opinions into the story, which would be fine if they didn't do it under the guise of fair and impartial journalism. They will shower praise on the shittiest, middle-of-the-road comics because they can safely show their clips. Also, every pseudodocumentary has to have the ethnic angle; what comics of what race have to overcome what obstacles. Fuck you. They're just uncircumcised hacks who overemphasize their accents to boost up weak, shitty jokes.

So after the Cellar, I head home and order egg whites and a lovely fresh fruit salad. I go to bed at seven in the morning, then toss and turn like a fucking rat for three hours because the sugar in the goddamn fruit was keeping me awake. I finally dozed off and got up today around 5:30. I really am starting to exist like a vampire with a heroin habit and it's disgusting me. I just took some Alka Seltzer Nighttime Cough and Cold shit so I should be off soon.

Now in addition to my pink eye and sore throat I have a cough and stuffy nose. I *hate* my sinuses; they've been a source of torture my entire life. My cunting septum is shaped like the Murrah Federal Building after Timothy McVeigh got through with it. However, the joys of laying in bed and digging for boogers, a.k.a. snacks, is very underrated. What better feeling then to scrape your nail into one and slowly guide it out? It looks like a cornflake with bloody porridge on it. Most boogers taste salty and have the consistency of rubber cement. I hate when you pop a nice one into your mouth and it gets caught in your teeth; it totally takes the joy out of eating it. Instead, it makes you feel like a vile, disgusting adult who's destined to spending eternity picking nose dirt out of their molars.

COINS

I'VE SPENT THE last week and a half trying to get a set on video that's four and a half minutes long. Ross from *The Tonight Show* called and requested the tape, and it really is hard to do that short a set. Most bits I do require me to make at least two minutes of funny faces and nutty hand gestures before I say a word. Eventually, I got a tolerable set at the Comic Strip and sent it off. There are obviously no guarantees but it's still nice that they're showing any interest at all. I'm sure within a week I'll be rejected and a Brazilian vomit-fetish film will be taped over my stupid act. One of the major problems I have with doing television is that my material content is *atrocious*. Not necessarily profanity (instead of "cunt," I use the euphemism "smelly Mr. Ed lips," or I just hold my nose, point at my crotch and refer to it as her "you-know-what") but still unpleasant enough to be exiled to cable.

I also got a call today from the guy who sold my merchandise when I performed at the Bonnaroo festival. I sold two CDs and one DVD. Three goddamn items?? Hitler sold more swag in Rockaway. I fucking stink. The man said that no comedy stuff sold and part of the problem was that it wasn't sold in the comedy tent, but at another tent across the compound. Not only did I not make a profit on the merchandise, but I lost money on the shipping. My boxes will be sent home weighing almost exactly the same as when they left, and there's something truly enraging about that.

Besides thinking about the tape for Ross, most of my last three days has revolved around rolling coins. In my closet I had a shitload of plastic cups and a pillowcase half filled with change. The pillowcase I've had since

I lived in New Jersey and have just been too lazy to do anything with it. To clear a bit of room in my closet I decided to buy one of those automatic coin sorters and get started. The first coin sorter I bought looked relatively sturdy and cost me $50. It not only sorted the coins and put them into the proper coin sleeves but gave you a constant read out of how much money you've put through it. The description on the stupid box neglected to mention how easily pennies jam up the machine. Whenever you put a bunch of pennies in, the cocksucking thing clogs up and stops. I finally wound up punching it a few times to loosen the clogged pennies and then just wound up assaulting it. It felt wonderful to break that jammed-up, plastic piece of dogshit.

The only problem was that now I have all these coins and no way to sort them. I certainly had no intention of doing it by hand like someone's grandmother. So what do I do? Run out and buy the exact same coin sorter I had just broken and thrown out. I rushed home with my new sorter, opened the box, and promptly dropped it on the floor. The whole front of it cracked in half. I almost picked it up and hurled it through my bedroom window. I turned it on and, to my shock, it was operational. I spent the next few hours finishing up and writing my stupid account number on *every* roll. I'm glad I called the bank first, because if I'd have just shown up with a duffel bag of change and was told I had to write something on every sleeve right there in the bank line, I'd have put a roll of quarters in my fist and broken that bitch's jaw. By the way, the final tally was $697 worth of change. I couldn't fucking believe it. I've been tossing it into those stupid cups and pillowcase for so long it really added up. That's enough for two really good, or six really lousy, blowjobs.

THE BIG COLLECTION

I FINISHED THE week at the Stress Factory last night. After the show, instead of enjoying the oral favors of an adoring gal (or even a gal who hates me but is afraid of a gun), I had to go to my parent's house and clean out shit that I've had stored there for years because they're moving (it was in this very house I began my infamous collection of coins). Most of the things are just personal nonsense I've collected, nothing really of substance. The problem is, I save *everything*; one box will have family photos and the next will have a brick that was once hurled at me by a minority. It's hard to distinguish between the worthwhile stuff and the absolute garbage. The one thing I was most psyched about was my baseball card collection. I started it when I was a kid, then resumed it in the early nineties for a year or so. I haven't even looked at them in about twelve years. There are still too many of them to bring to my apartment in one trip, but I brought the special ones, which I had put into protective plastic holders years ago. Also, I had three full special card-holding notebooks. The other huge boxes I left for another trip; this first haul would focus on the real gems.

The worst thing for me about cleaning out my old room was having my parents lurking there, talking to me. Not that I mind talking to them, I was just afraid that while perusing an old box in my closet I'd come across a batch of animal porn or something else that makes me want to jerk off. Hard to find a rational explanation when you're chatting with your parents and you yank out a glossy magazine with some guy in big sunglasses fucking a donkey on the cover. So I shooed them out of the room and continued rummaging through my closet. I found old Ozzy concert T-shirts, and I'd love to know when I was ever small enough to fit into them. I tried one on (executioner holding Ozzy's severed head) and it fit me like a dickie. I felt like an old, out of shape slob, so I reluctantly threw it away, along with a lot of other clothes that were decidedly awful. No wonder I had trouble getting girls. Considering the clothing I used to wear it's a miracle I wasn't forced to fuck turtles and geese until I stumbled onto prostitution.

I did come across a shirt I got from Shane McMahon's bachelor party (I opened for Bob Levy and bombed horribly. Vince wouldn't even make eye contact with me.) and a Laker windbreaker I am fond of. I also found artwork, things I drew throughout my life. As a kid I wanted to be an artist; looking back, I have no idea why. I cannot see one iota of artistic potential or talent in any of the drawings. Most of my drawings look like something a Parkinson's patient would scribble on paper while holding the pen in their trembling assholes. I guess I listened to my mom's encouraging words like an idiot. I probably made a turkey by tracing my hand when I was four and she told me I was good and from then on I thought I had a rare gift.

One of the better things I found was a trophy I got in 1993. It was the comedy portion of a Black History Month contest and I won. The only other white guy in the building was another comic who ate his balls horribly. At that point, I had been doing comedy for about three years; I think I took off my shirt and put on a goofy hat and did something else racially humiliating. They probably gave me the trophy to be merciful. I will proudly display it in my apartment just to irritate black people when they come over.

So I finally get home around three in the morning and promptly treat myself to some not-so-inexpensive sex. After she fakes an orgasm with all the conviction of Sandra Bullock doing Shakespeare, she leaves and I shower. Once again, no fucking hot water so I am washing my already tiny nuts in a freezing shower. I get out and sit down at my computer and join an online baseball card pricing site. Finally, I can look them up, check out what I've been sitting on all these years. I joined the baseball, football, and basketball card sites as I had cards from all three sports that I deemed valuable. After two hours of checking and pulling cards out of boxes I have come to the conclusion that my card collection is virtually worthless. I have a Bill Bradley card from the mid-seventies and it's only worth ten bucks. *TEN FUCKING DOLLARS?* This cocksucker was a senator. And my O.J. Simpson card from around that time is worth the same thing. I never realized lopping off a woman's head drags down your memorabilia value so much. A few of my baseball cards were in the $40 to $80 range, but that's only a few and they're not in the perfect condition needed to merit the higher value. Serves me right; you should have seen me traipsing down the hallway with boxes clenched protectively against my fat tits; I really thought I had a little gold mine on my hands.

Even after realizing that things I've saved since 1979 are the collectable equivalent of mouse shit, I still refused to throw them out. So a couple of hours ago I schlepped out to Manhattan Mini Storage and rented a bin to store them in. Fifty-eight fucking dollars a month (insurance is mandatory). So I go back home only to find out that my apartment had free storage in the basement. I spent money to store something worthless and I could have done it for free. I then bought an omelet with bacon and a blueberry muffin because those things sit nicely in your stomach when you're going to bed at noon.

The only bit of good news is that my pink eye is gone. I don't want to feel too good about that, though, because with my luck it's only gone because AIDS scared it off.

This is me. Holding flowers makes me feel giddy and light-hearted.

BOO!

IT'S HALLOWEEN EVENING and gratefully, this silly holiday will be over soon. Today has been filled with ring after ring of the doorbell, a parade of little costumes, and trying to discreetly slip razor blades into apples and candy bars. And while it's a repetitious, draining day of running back and forth, the look on a youngster's face when I answer the door with a handful of treats and my robe wide open makes it all worthwhile. This year's costumes have been quite varied; everything from *Scream* movie masks to the ever popular Little Conner Peterson (blue face, wet clothes, and a hat made of placenta). There were so many good ones, picking a favorite may be impossible. There was the little black girl with lemonade on her face who was dressed as R. Kelly's toilet, the boy with Down's syndrome who painted red stitching on his face and went as Mr. Met, and the svelte, almost-teenage lad who wore white pants with a big ketchup stain on the back and went as a Michael Jackson houseguest. I admired their creativity and had no patience for the bad boys and girls with plain, store-bought costumes.

Due to time constraints I will leave out details, but rest assured I administered quite a few bare-bottom spankings to lazy trick-or-treaters. I also had no patience for punks who refused to say, "Trick or Treat." When I was a boy, every door we knocked on got the mantra of, "Trick or treat, smell my feet, give me something good to eat!" As an adult I look back on this rhyme and find it to be incomprehensibly irritating, and if I heard a child reciting it in a sing-song voice I'd probably bite his shitty little fingers off. However, for pedophiles, having children knock on the door, ask for candy, and offer a good foot-sniffing must make for a fine afternoon. As a condition of their parole, most kid touchers are not allowed to open the door for trick-or-treaters. Jesus, that must be torture. All of those hairless, supple hineys on the other side of the door, ring-a-ding-dinging your bell all day long, "Could we have thum candy mithter?" You're forced to just wrap your cock in marshmallows and jerk off, leering at them through the letter slot.

I never quite understood pedophilia; I hate being around kids, I can't comprehend wanting to fuck one of those little monsters. First of all, their hands are always sticky. And even worse than fucking them is that afterward, you have to be nice so they don't rat you out to the whole goddamn neighborhood. "I know, you little shit, I know . . . ice cream for breakfast again." Sounds like too much work to me. If you like smooth and hairless so much, why not just fuck Asians or cancer patients?

More important, the key to a successful Halloween is to have things the kids will love. This year I armed myself with an array of popular treats; everything from sardines to yamsicles to cod-liver oil, with the occasional lucky little tot getting a German shit film thrown into their treat bag. At certain points during the day I even gave the rascally revelers a good scare by answering the door in my Shrek mask and giving an evil laugh, "Mu-hahahaha, mu-hahahaha." Those who were legitimately scared received a good-natured pat on the head and a treat, those who made smart-alecky remarks received a face full of scalding coffee from the pot I kept by the door. I switched outfits periodically during the day, even sending a couple of five-year-olds into gales of laughter by putting on my Robert Reed wig, pricking my finger, and threatening to bleed on them. They were quite hip for five-year-olds, and one of them even gave me a hearty laugh by throwing out a Cousin Oliver/fisting reference.

Unfortunately, not all of the day's encounters were filled with laughter and mirth and me fighting an erection. There was one case that was downright sad. My bell rang and a mother stood there with her two small children, ages four and six. The mom was almost in tears when she said that she just didn't have the money to buy costumes, and would I mind giving the kids some candy anyway? They looked embarrassed and hungry as their joyless little eyes looked up at me, silently pleading. All kidding aside, slamming the door in their faces and threatening to call the police is one of the hardest things I've had to do in weeks. I felt it was the best course of action, though, as the kids were probably too young to understand that their mother had small, droopy tits and was therefore in no position to ask for favors from anyone.

The events of the day invariably brought me back to my own childhood and many years of trick-or-treating. One year, I am guessing around fourth or fifth grade, I thought it would be funny to knock on people's doors and say, "We's just a tricksen and a treatsen!" I don't know why I thought that was funny, at that age I probably wasn't aware that I was doing a degrading parody of the American Negro (which is, of course, what makes it such a rib-tickler in hindsight). As a boy I frequently made up awful, spine-curdling words like that. For instance, I would at times refer to a pocketbook as a "purse-abook" and police officers as "Mr. Copperpoliceman." The more I delve into my childhood, the more I realize that I was almost always a weirdo.

Another fine Halloween memory occurred when I was about twelve and was tricksen-and-treatsen with my friend Marvin. We rang one bell and the gentleman said through the door that he was sorry, but he didn't have any candy. This prompted Marvin to put his chewing gum over the peephole of the man's door. This in turn prompted the man, a foreigner, to run outside, put Marvin in a headlock, and punch the top of his head. I stood there impotently as good old Marv took knuckle sandwich after knuckle sandwich to the skull. I was never big on jumping in to protect my friends when I was a boy. Several years before that, my friend Bruce and I were playing at my house. We were having a fine time until some of my other friends came over and decided they didn't like Bruce. They began pelting him with those odd, awful red berries that only grow on apartment complex shrubs. Bruce was crying and frightened and I didn't help matters when I jumped on the bandwagon and began pelting him right along with them.

I don't necessarily fault myself for this childhood lack of loyalty. One of my earliest memories revolves around being left out to dry by one of my stupid friends. I've always had weird feelings about the vagina—fear of it at times, and I can trace a lot of that back to an instance that occurred at the pool of my apartment complex. I was maybe five years old. We were sitting on blankets next to a woman whose name I don't remember, but I do recall she was dating the superintendent of the complex. I was staring between her legs because pubic hair was bulging out the sides of her bathing suit. I leaned over to Tony and whispered that I could see some hairs. Back in those days, my whispering skills must have left something to be desired, because she popped her awful face out of her magazine and menacingly asked, "What did you just say?" Even at that age I realized the tone of her voice implied she'd heard *exactly* what I just said and was making a quick confirmation. I replied, "Nothing," and stupid fucking Tony blurts out that I said I could see hairs. He ratted me out. She bolted up and screamed, "You little fucking pig! Get out of here and I don't want to see you again." Everyone looked and I ran away from the pool, humiliated. I don't know whatever happened to that cunt of a woman, but to this day I'd like to strangle her with a shoelace. No wonder I only like shame sex and break into a cold sweat every time I look at a vagina. The only good news is that a couple of years later, the guy she was dating backed a lawn mower over his foot and severed two toes.

I can also look back to this time as the origin of my awful, dysfunctional cycle with women. For some reason when I like a girl, and I mean really like her, I can only stand at a distance and admire. I cannot approach her; I almost like the fantasy of being her boyfriend more than the potential reality. Once again, I was maybe five or six years old, still living in Edison, and there was a girl who lived down the hill with whom I guess you can say I was in puppy love. I don't remember her name or her face; only how I felt about her. One day my parents explained to me that she was moving away and I wouldn't see her anymore. My mom put out some folded clothes for me on the bed and told me to get dressed so I could go down the hill and say good-bye to her. A pattern of my life has been to detach and become paralyzed emotionally when it comes to women and it probably started on that very day. As the day wore on, and it was getting later and later, my mom kept telling me to go down the hill to see her. I buried my stupid head in the sand, figuring if I didn't acknowledge that she was leaving, then it wouldn't be true. Hours later I got dressed and went down the hill only to be told that her family had already left. I looked in her apartment and it was empty; just a few scattered empty boxes and marks on the wall where pictures had been hung. I never saw her again. For some reason that day has always stuck with me, and while I cannot remember what I wore on Friday, I have never forgotten that folded pile of clothes on my bed.

As I glance back over this little ditty it's obvious I've gotten off track. Maybe next year for Halloween I can wear a bedsheet over my body, put a pile of folded clothes on my head, and go to parties dressed as a boring, melodramatic story. The line is sometimes blurry between "opening up and letting people know who you are" and "another jerkoff whining about his childhood." This was supposed to be a tale of ghosts and goblins, and I've turned it into a pseudointrospective sleep inducer.

In all of my ramblings, I forgot to mention the youngster who rang my bell today wearing a gorilla costume with a Barbie doll taped to his shoulder. He also had a small airplane in his hand. I asked the little fellow who he was supposed to be and he responded, "King Kong, you fucking faggot," and then kicked me in the balls and took my dish full of candy.

1987 LETTER I WROTE TO A GIRL I WAS DATING

THIS IS AN actual letter that I wrote in 1987. I was dating a girl for a short while and I decided to bang my ex-girlfriend, who had hooked us up to begin with. My ex told my current girlfriend that we fucked and tossed a monkey wrench into this new situation. I've transcribed the letter, complete with spelling mistakes. I haven't changed a word. My critique, done today, is in italics. I am just amazed at what a completely phony asshole I was. I got caught cheating then decided to try pop psychology 101. The girl I cheated on did read this letter and left it at my house, which is why I still have it.

D——,   8-19-87

Well, I read your letter and it was basically what I expected. As far as changing your thinking, forget It I'm not trying to. *Changing her thinking is precisely what I was trying to do.* Let me tell you a couple of things. *Look out, bitch; a real man is about to be assertive!* First of all, I didn't say to J—— that you were naked, I said you didn't have a shirt on. Not a big difference, but a difference none the less. *A minuscule, nitpicky difference would have been more accurate. Anytime you have to revert to semantics three lines into an explanation letter, you're in deep shit.* And your not looking for too much, you're just not accepting the reasons being given and that's on you. If you think I'm just sweet talking you now with fancy explanations and reasonings, think again. *Think again, even though you're completely correct.* Let me tell you something, I don't sweat any goddamn body, I don't

63

care who they are. *Not only is this a pathetic suburban attempt at sounding black, it is a fucking lie. I've sweated* countless *people and will undoubtedly continue to do so.* And I've also looked worse than I do now, I mean I've felt humiliated back in the day. *An even more pathetic attempt at urban hipness.* There's no reason to bullshit you now. *Except for the fact that I'd like to continue fucking you.*

Also, M—— didn't tell you what she did because of you being supposedly gullible, you know why she told you. (unless you think I bullshitted you on the bench the other day, in which case you have no idea) If you actually think that I took part in what happened to make you look stupid, gullible etc., or that I didn't feel badly about what happened, you have no idea what you're talking about. Despite what happened, no-one can fucking tell <u>me</u> how <u>I</u> feel. *Aaaahhhhh, yes. Underlining. Not only does it punctuate a point, but it screams* **I AM LYING! I AM LYING!** I almost drank over what happened. *Perhaps the most manipulative thing I have ever thought, much less written. What a transparent worm I was.* "Well then why did you keep doing it?" *Another telltale sign you are a lying sack of shit; anticipating the person's response, surrounding it with quotes, and then answering in the next sentence.* Those are reasons you can't or just don't want to see. And if you think that's a cop-out, so what, think it. *If she didn't think it was a cop-out, then she was an even bigger fucking dummy than I thought she was.*

By the way, I do know what it's like to care about people. *That's right baby; this tiger has a tough exterior but a heart of gold.* In my addiction I hurt the people I love the most, and sometimes I still hurt people I care about. *See? When I fucked my ex the other day, it was all a part of my addiction. I'm not a **bad** person trying to get good; I'm a **sick** person trying to get well! Bleeechhh; how revolting.* I don't use alcoholism as an excuse, but the personality traits and character defects that come with it <u>do</u>

dictate some of my actions, reasonings, justifications, etc. *Dickhead move number 734: State how you don't use something as an excuse, then proceed to do exactly that. And don't forget to underline.* I have no reason to bullshit now, because what happened is out in the open. Do you honestly think I would go against what my sponsor told me and jepordize my sobriety just to make a fool out of you? *Don't you understand? My* LIFE *is at stake here! What a disingenuous, melodramatic douche I was.*

I'm not saying it was right, it was deceitful and wrong, and I'm not defending it. I'm also not trying to get you to say, "Poor Jim almost drank." *I wasn't?* I did what I did with knowledge of what the consequences might be, I'm only saying that there are things involved you don't understand, that's all. *Apparently I thought that "My cock felt great in my ex-girlfriend's snatch," was too deep a concept for this girl to grasp.* It's not so plain and obvious like you think. *This is a complex situation; me dumping a load all over her is but a symptom of this insidious problem.*

Mabey you don't know how much I really like you. *I didn't enjoy eating her ass and teabagging her; I did it for* us. If you think that's bullshit, fine. I told you time and time again before you knew about me & M—— how smart I think you are. I <u>never</u> took you for a fool. *I also never took you for a private detective either, you nosey twat.* I've deceived teachers and psychologists before, and they are quite intelligent people. Because you don't know something is happening, it's not a reflection on your intelligence. *The granddaddy of all bullshit; it's not that you're so dumb, it's just that I'm so smart. I got over on you but don't feel bad, toots, you're in good company. As soon as she read this she should have eviscerated me with a sewing needle.*

What I did hurt you and <u>was</u> fucked up, and I'm sorry for lying to you. Believe me or don't. If I didn't care or regret it, I would have told you to fuck off when you confronted me, and you can believe that. *Or maybe I wouldn't have told you to fuck off, maybe I just would have lied and squirmed to your face instead of doing it on paper.*

I've said enough, I personally don't care if anybody believes a word I say. *Not only do I care if you believe me, but since you're a hot girl who was willing to fuck me, I am begging you to believe me.* If it will take time for you to trust and believe me again, that's fine, if you never do, then don't, shit. *Who is this intriguing young ghetto hipster? He sure grovels a lot for someone who's indifferent.* I <u>am</u> very sorry for everything, there are still things I have to change in myself. I never claimed to be a fucking saint. I hope you can understand what I've tried to tell you in this letter, if not, then keep thinking whatever the fuck it is you're thinking now. *A very convincing way to end the letter. Always make your final sentences have the tone and cadence of a union dock worker who just lost a card game. "Smarten up, cunt face," would've had a more romantic lilt to it.*

Jim

8-19-87

Well, I read your letter and it was basically what I expected. As far as changing your thinking, forget it. I'm not trying to. Let me tell you a couple of things. First of all, I didn't say to ~~████~~ that you were naked, I said you didn't have a shirt on. Not a big difference, but there's a difference more the less. And your not looking for too much, you're just not accepting the reasons being given, and that's on you. If you think I'm just sweet talking you now with fancy explanations and reasonings, think again. Let me tell you something, I don't sweat my goddamn body, I don't care who they are. And I've also looked worse than I do now, I mean I've felt humiliated back in the day. There is no reason to bullshit you now.

Also, ~~████~~ didn't tell you what she did because of your very supposedly gullible, you know why she told you. (Unless you think I bullshitted you on the bench the other day, in which case you have no idea.) If you actually think that I took part in what happened to make you look stupid, gullible etc., or that I didn't feel badly about what happened, you have no idea what you're talking about. Despite what happened, no one can fucking tell me how I feel. I almost don't even know what happened. "Well then why did you keep doing it?" There are reasons you can't or just don't want to see. And if you think that's a cop-out, so what, think it.

By the way, I do know what it's like to care about people. In my addiction I hurt the people I love most, and something I tell hurt people I care about. I don't use alcoholism as an excuse, but the personality traits and character defects that come with it do dictate some of my actions, reasonings, justifications, etc. I have no reason to bullshit now, because what happened is out in the open. Do you honestly think I would go against what my sponsor told me and jeopardize

67

my sobriety just ~~for~~ to make a fool out of you?

I'm not saying it was right, it was deceitful and wrong, and I'm not defending it. I'm also not trying to get you to say "Poor Jim almost drank". I did what I did with knowledge of what the consequences might be. I'm only saying that there are things involved you don't understand, that's all. It's not so plain and obvious like you think.

Maybe you don't know how much I really like you if you think that's bullshit, fine. I told you time and time again before you knew about me & ~~[scratched out]~~ how smart I think you are. I never took you for a fool. I've deceived teachers and psychologists before, and they are quite intelligent people. Because you don't know something is happening, it's not a reflection on your intelligence.

What I did hurt you and was fucked up, and I'm sorry for lying to you. Believe me I do. If I didn't care or regret it, I would have told you to fuck off when you confronted me, and you can believe that.

I've said enough, I personally don't care if anybody believes a word I say. If it will take time for you to trust and believe me again, that is fine, if you never do, then don't, shit. I am very sorry for everything, there are still things I have to change in myself. I never claimed to be a fucking saint. I hope you can understand what I've tried to tell you in this letter, if not, then keep thinking whatever the fuck it is you're thinking now.

The scribblings of a melodramatic, suburban cracker.

JOE PESKY

I WAS AT the Comedy Cellar last night, and word got out that Joe Pesci (my mother always mispronounced his last name as "Pesky") was next door at Café Wha? with Kevin James. I don't know how they are acquainted; maybe Joe is playing a rapist on an upcoming *King of Queens* episode. I know Kevin casually, although it's been years since I've spoken with him. He and Joe were ready to get into a car and leave, and my friend Hatem and I nervously slinked up to them and the people they were with. Pesci saw me coming and got in the car; I guess the camera I already had open didn't help.

I fired out an awkward, insincere, horseshit of a "Hello," to Kevin, who was much nicer to me than I would've been to some starstruck dolt in that situation. I skipped the pleasantries and mentioned I wanted a picture with Joe. Instead of spitting in my fucking face to teach me some manners, Kevin actually leaned in the car and told Joe that I was a good friend and a nice guy. Pesci said no problem, got out of the car, and I got my shot. As he stood next to me, I had to say something, so I bumbled out, "I loved you in *Goodfellas*." Pesci grunts what could be somehow interpreted as a thank you. What a dumb fucking *cunt* I am. Could I have possibly picked a more trite, hacky thing to say? I should have mentioned *JFK* or even *Raging Bull*, but fucking *Goodfellas*? I would have come off better if I had hit him on the arm, called him a "stuttering prick," and then eagerly waited for him to laugh. He got back in the car immediately.

I then had to shake Kevin's hand and avoid eye contact because we both know that was a fine example of the different worlds we live in.

Joe Pesci, thanks to Kevin James.

ANOTHER SILLY SITCOM IDEA

I WAS ON the toilet this afternoon reading a copy of *Harper's Bazaar* and shitting a stewlike concoction. I began thinking of another sitcom to write and I got so engrossed in thought that it took me twenty minutes to realize that the lid was down and my pants were still on. I laughed good-naturedly at my error and decided against cleaning up in favor of a nice nap.

The show I was milling about in my mind would be a family-oriented comedy. I want to play a father, some sort of blue-collar worker who is married to a black woman (I feel that interracial relationships have a place in modern television, and I also like the idea of nicknaming her "the lazy African"). We would live somewhere in the suburbs and have a white picket fence and two cars in the garage. I would be a plumber or carpenter and she would either be a waitress or work as a fluffer on nonunion snuff films. We would have two adopted children named Timmy and Jimmy, both girls. As episodes progressed it would be revealed that we adopted because she had a hysterectomy to settle a football wager she lost. Timmy and Jimmy would not only be twins but they'd both be mischevious little scamps. Every episode would have one of the rascals drinking cleaning products or accidentally murdering a puppy while attempting to pet it with a hammer. I'd come home to my black wife and stupid adopted children every day and be so frustrated that one of the running jokes would be me muttering, "I'm tempted to burn a cross on my own doggone lawn, for Pete's sake."

It's the frustration of Lemar (my character) that people would relate to. He deals with the issues that plague most modern men; being a working stiff who is unable to get ahead, frustration with the government, and most important, a maddening desire to molest the paper boy. Of course at one point, his wife's pesky mother would have to come for a visit. Not only do she and Lemar not like each other, but she's a wheelchair-bound invalid. Whenever Uhnga (Lemar's wife) leaves the room, he runs over to the mother and tosses dried cat shit into her open mouth. There is an understanding that she was against the wedding from the get-go, not only because of the racial difference, but because Lemar is HIV positive and has webbed feet. Uhnga has a son from a previous marriage who was arrested for possession of a stolen coat and pleaded it down to raping a nun with a cheerleading baton. Lemar's family is the polar opposite of the Johnsons. They are accepting and ultraliberal in all areas of life, except when dealing with faggots and Jews. ("Any man who will put a cock in his mouth don't have sense enough to vote correctly," Lemar's father was fond of saying.)

The real test of this modern-day family will be to see how well they hold up to the pressures of daily life. Do the additional challenges they face enhance and strengthen their love, or do they resort to beating each other with frying pans while shouting things like, "Nigger," and, "Duck-footed white motherfucker"? Do the children learn and slowly progress, or do they degenerate to a point of such irritating helplessness that even doctors and psychologists want to drown them in a bathtub like kittens? Will Uhnga ever have enough money to get her female plumbing back from loan sharks so she and Lemar can have their own half-breed, mongrel child? It's questions like these that I believe will fuel the first season and leave the public starving for the second.

I do realize that conceptually, this is all a bit cutesy and I am indeed searching for ways to spice it up a bit. Friends and family have offered suggestions ranging from having the children nude in every scene to making Lemar a locomotive engineer just so I can name the show *Cleveland Steamer*. While these ideas and many others I've gotten are all enticing in their own way, I feel it's important to stay away from overly cheap and tawdry ideas. There are only so many TV-friendly shit jokes you can make (1,406 is the estimate most people are comfortable with) and after a few seasons people will tire of them. Again, this is still a work in progress, so please don't judge too harshly.

PUMPKIN, A LOVE STORY

"PUMPKIN, A LOVE Story" is an odd one to say the least. It was written almost eight years ago and cost me a three-year relationship. And I don't mean that vaguely, I mean it literally; my girlfriend of three years called me in tears and dumped me, which really hurt because I had written it for her. Looking back on this I cannot actually believe I expected her to laugh (I still think it's pretty funny, just not when written for a girlfriend).

This invention revolves around the Man (yours truly) and Pumpkin (my beloved). Pumpkin was my actual nickname for her. She was one of the funnier people I have dated; the problem is, I never told her how much certain things made me laugh. One thing she'd do is hug me in public and jog in place while we embraced. She did it just to embarrass me and it worked like a charm. I would always act like I hated it, but in all honesty I thought it was hilarious; it was one of my favorite things she did. You'll notice a lot of barbarism in the humor (what else is new) and that's what really freaked her out. I thought she'd understand where it was coming from but instead she just thought I was a piece of shit and that was that. It's one of the few things I regret writing because it didn't represent the way I felt about her. There was no hidden anger seeping out, this was purely done to be funny. Actually, it's the handing it over to her part I regret. Jesus, I was an ass.

It's a hot day in July; 98 degrees, humid, and the Man is waiting impatiently on the corner. He looks at his watch again, wondering when this fucking bitch is gonna get here. He doesn't mind waiting sometimes, there's a lot of hot pussy to look at here in the Big Apple. The Man has his eye on some black broad's ass (he normally doesn't go for blacks, but this broad looks like she was just built for fucking) when he hears an annoying and familiar sound from the middle of the crowd. "Meep, meep. Meep, meep." The Man feels his fist balling up. Every time he hears this "meep meep" shit, he wants to knock out two or three of this bitch's teeth and put her in the hospital. He knows he can't do that; the judge said one more assault on a woman and he was going back up the river. (Not that Pumpkin knew any of this, and probably wouldn't have believed it if she did.) "Maybe I can make it look like an accident . . ." His thoughts are interrupted as he is jolted back into reality. "Meep meep, Pumpkin comin' through!" People begin to move about, trying to clear a path. "Meep, meep, 'scuse me, guys, there's a Pumpkin comin' through." The Man sees her approaching, head down, doing that stupid walk/jog-in-place-type shuffle she does. She spots the Man, and her face breaks out into a moronic grin. "Hi, honey! I hope you weren't waiting long, I had to make a quick stop in the bathroom." What else is new. This broad shits like a goose eating Mexican food; the Man never met a chick who spent so much time on the bowl. Before he could say a word, she chimed in with, "Punkin hadda go to da baffroom and make Punkin seeds," which makes the Man want to vomit and crack her skull open all in one motion.

The Man can't do either of these things, though; he needs her for something, so he just forces a big smile and says, "No, Pumpkin, I wasn't waiting long. Not long at all."

The ten-block walk back to the car is an exquisite kind of torture. The sun is relentlessly beating down on the Man's head, his feet are sore, and he has a rectal itch that should be entered into the *Guinness Book of World Records*. (Earlier that day, the Man was masturbating with a pretzel rod in his anus. The combination of salt, sweat, and chafing has made his backside an amusement park of discomfort. He makes a mental note to try unsalted rods.) To top it all off, Pumpkin is prattling on incessantly about her day. "And then <u>he</u> said, blah blah blah. So I look at her and go, blah blah blah." The Man is interjecting an occasional, "Really, honey?" and "Wow, that's interesting!" but is all the while thinking how nice it would be to shut her the fuck up by cramming his sweaty man meat into her Pumpkiny yapper.

They finally make it back to the car after two additional stops in the toilet for Ms. Cancer Colon. There's traffic leaving the Lincoln Tunnel, and if she has to take another dump, she may just have to hang her fat ass out the window and shit all over the 495 helix. The thought of this makes the Man chortle with delight. "What's so funny, sweetie?" He doesn't answer, and is annoyingly prompted again, "Come on honey, tell me! Tell me the joke! Pumpkin likes jokes!" The Man looks at her and smiles good-naturedly (smiling now is easy, he's picturing Pumpkin's head with the claw end of a hammer buried in it). "I was just thinking about that time we were in the park and I stepped in poop. Remember how we both had such a laugh over that one! Our first picnic, and me with a sneaker full of poop." Pumpkin squeals with delight, "Yes, I remember that! It was our first date! You hopping around on one foot and me calling you Mr. Poopy Shoes!" This sends Pumpkin into gales of laughter, and the Man smiles along. He remembers that day well, because he had taken Pumpkin to the park with the sole intention of raping her. They were walking to "the spot," when he set his foot down in a moist pile of fresh, butterscotch-colored dog shit. As he lifted his brand new white Adidas hightop to survey the damage, she is laughing and pointing and calling him Mr. Poopy Shoes. The Man had to physically restrain himself from grabbing that squawking bitch by the hair and scraping his shitty shoe against her teeth. She was laughing so hard and leaping about, he was afraid she would drop the picnic basket and all the fried chicken and chloroform would fall out of it. Then she suddenly threw her arms around him and gave him a hug. "Don't worry, Pumpkin still likes you, Mr. Poopy Shoes," and kissed him on the cheek. Again the Man thought of cleaning his shoe on her face and raping her, but instead just gritted his teeth and said, "Thanks."

The rest of the ride home isn't bad; she has finally realized he's ignoring her and shut up. Inside, though, his wheels are turning. Her parents just got her a new car. If he can get his hands on it and sell it, he can pay off a couple of debts. The trick is to be nice to her, and then ask to borrow it. He's not worried about the police; he'll just tell them a nigger stole it. He brilliantly begins to plant the seed, "This damn car isn't running right, and I have to work tonight. Motherfucker!" He slams his fist on the wheel to drive home the point. "I'm afraid if I drive this thing tonight, I'll be killed. Oh well, who'll care? As long as my Pumpkin is safe, I'm happy." Pumpkin, visibly alarmed, looks at the Man. "Oh, honey, you'll do no such thing! Please, take my car tonight; I'll cancel that stupid concert." The Man is secretly wondering how Pumpkin's platoon of dyke friends will react to that news. "No, Pumpkin, I couldn't let you do that. I want you to have fun tonight. Don't you worry about l'il old me, I'll be okay . . . I guess." "No sweetie, I insist! I'll just have to call blah blah blah . . ." He has stopped listening already. She's gonna cancel her show? No shit, Sherlock. If she didn't, he would've planted his foot so far in her box, she'd have been calling him Mr. Pussy Shoes. This thought makes the Man chortle all over again, and the thought of her box gives him a stirring in his undershorts, which he squeezes roughly. "Maybe I'll get some relief for this puppy before I go out," thinks the Man as he pulls into the driveway.

Once inside the house, it's time to put Phase 2 of the plan into action. He hands Pumpkin the phone. The first friend she has to call is some poetry-writing bitch, who the Man hates[1]. She's a bad influence

---

1. She did have a new friend who wrote poetry. I complained to my girl about her because I thought she was badmouthing me. I was probably right.

on Pumpkin, always trying to get her to go to clubs, drink, and suck off minorities. Pumpkin denies this, but the Man knows; he may have been born at night, but he wasn't born *last* night! Besides, he's read her poetry, and it doesn't rhyme. "If it don't rhyme, it ain't poetry," is what the Man always says. After she makes her calls and cancels her plans (and unknowingly saves herself a punch in the tits), Pumpkin calls her parents. The Man doesn't mind this, because Pumpkin's parents adore him. They always tell her that if she stopped bellyaching and acted more like him, she'd be fine. This advice sits nicely with the Man, thank you very much. After calling her folks, Pumpkin asks the Man if he'd like to go to the bedroom. He grabs his blood-engorged pole through his Sport-a-bouts and says, "Whadda you think, stupid?" This masculine attitude never fails to get Pumpkin's baby maker all nice and slippery, and she gleefully hustles into the room. "I'll be right in Pumpkin, I gotta pinch a loaf," calls out the Man. After depositing a couple of eggplant sized logs into the crapper, he dollops a thumb full of Vaseline into his shit vent to ease the itching. Now he's ready for a little tonsil hockey and some ass sex. Once he's inside the room, Pumpkin jumps up to greet him. "Could Pumpkin have a hug first?" Truth be known, he'd rather hug her throat with a telephone cord, but considering his need for that car (not to mention a little stinky on his hang down)[2] the Man generously opens his arms. As he's hugging her, he feels her head moving back and forth. "Oh, fuck, not this fucking shit!" thinks the Man. Pumpkin, while hugging the Man, is slowly jogging in place, something she does subconsciously when she's overly excited. Sex is out of the question now; this jogging crap always makes his prick shrink like it was exposed to radiation. Sometimes when she's doing it, he steps on her foot really hard and pretends it was an accident. He decides to be

---

2. "Stinky on his hangdown" is an Otto & George line I stole. Give me a fucking break; I wrote this hoping my girlfriend would chuckle and then blow me. I never dreamed I'd be publishing this stupid thing.

nice though; he doesn't need the hassle of beating her to get the car keys. The Man says he's no longer in the mood, and makes up an excuse about being on his period. Pumpkin, who makes up in the jugs for what she lacks in the brains department, believes it. Besides, later on while she's asleep, he can always sniff her panties and jerk off into her makeup kit. Pumpkin sheepishly hands over the keys, and pushes her forehead out for a little kiss goodnight. The man ignores her head, pinches her titty, and heads out the door to take care of business.

Twenty minutes later he's doing ninety on the turnpike with the windows up, enjoying the sour, meaty odor of his own farts. Now the Man's mind is organizing the night's events; first, he will stop in Jersey City to sell the car (he has already worked out a deal to get $500 for it), second, he will take a cab to L'il Kinney's place to pay him the $400 he owes him[3]. These first two steps are the most important. After that, he will probably call the police and say that two moolies stole his girlfriend's car. While he waits for the pigs, he'll use the $100 profit to buy some DVDs he's had his eye on. Next he'll call Pumpkin (if he can do it without laughing), and have her pick him up in his car, go to the cop shop, make a statement, then go home and fuck her in the mouth.

The Man has about an hour and a half before he's scheduled to drop off the car, so he decides to pull into a rest area and make some calls on Pumpkin's cell phone. His mind begins to wander, though, to the night he lost the $400 to L'il Kinney. L'il Kinney is the 6'5" leader of the G-Rajes, a vicious gang of black rapists. One night over drinks, L.K. was commenting on how he wouldn't mind "having a crack at Pumpkin's dumper," which the Man said could be arranged for $400. The Man tried casually mentioning it to her. "Hey baby, do you have any black in you? No? Would you like

3. L'il Kinney is a parking garage chain in NYC. The logo is this dopey-looking caricature, so to annoy her I always said that it was me they modeled the L'il Kinney logo after. And you couldn't possibly hate me reading this nearly as much as I hate myself for admitting it.

some?" Pumpkin never quite got the hint, and after every one of the Man's "funny jokes," she would throw her arms around him, kiss his cheek, and jog in place. He finally decided to scrap the idea; the last thing he needed was some nig stretching his personal supply out of shape. The problem was the money he had already taken from L'il Kinney; he'd spent it immediately on Ozzfest tickets and beer for himself and his buddies (not to mention two lap dances apiece after the show). The man glanced at his watch and decided to get a move on.

Again driving down the turnpike, the Man turned on the radio to catch the Yankees game; he had fifty bucks on the Yanks. If they lost, he may have to pawn Pumpkin's cell phone to cover the wager. When he turned on the radio, one of Pumpkin's CD's began to play. Normally when this happened, he would just throw it out the window, and if she asked any questions, just glare at her until she shut up. This CD was Ani DiFranco, a hairy-pitted carpet muncher the Man had a particular hatred for. But instead of tossing it, he just turned it down and began thinking of Pumpkin. She really was a pretty girl, and she was crazy about him. He found himself suddenly smiling thinking about her jog/hug, her little "Meep, Meep"s, her forehead, which needs lots of kisses, and her "Goin to da baffroom to make Punkin seeds." Out of nowhere, the Man felt an overwhelming cloud of guilt, and he began to cry. He felt guilty about wanting to murder her for giggling at his dookey shoe, guilty for stealing money out of her purse, for putting itching powder on her tampons. Guilty for calling her job anonymously and telling them that, "Pumpkin is a nigger lover." He wished he'd never stepped on her foot hard, ignored her stories, or made out with her father at that Fourth of July party. The Man suddenly wanted to hug and kiss Pumpkin, and he decided he was *not* going to sell her car or her phone, he had $8,000 in the bank, he would pay L'il Kinney with his own money! He turned off the turnpike to go to a bank machine.

Caught up in his thoughts, and in his rush to make it home and turn over a new leaf with Pumpkin, he didn't see the approaching headlights of the 18-wheeler. The last thought he had before he died was, "I hope Pumpkin's hungry, we're going out for a fancy dinner as soon as I get home," then looked up just in time to see the inside of his car illuminated, and the beginning of the CRASH . . .

The Man bolted upright in his car, breathing heavily and sweating. He'd fallen asleep at the rest area. He looked at the dashboard, the lights were glowing, and he could faintly hear Ani DiFranco playing through the speakers. As he pulled out of the rest area, he again thought of Pumpkin; of her smile, of her trusting eyes when she looked at him. He also thought about her mouth, and how he was going to brutally fuck it when he got home. He thought of this as he took the dyke out of the CD player, tossed her onto the highway, and gunned it back to ninety; L'il Kinney would be pissed if he was late with the money.

SLEEPY HEAD

TODAY STARTED OUT in a rather irritating fashion. Stress Factory owner Vinny Brand owed me a bit of cash from my engagement there. He was a good enough egg to agree to drive in today from central Jersey to give it to me around 2:00 p.m. I awoke promptly at 3:20 with that shitty, "I know I fucked up but I'm not sure how yet" feeling. As soon as I started listening to my messages I realized of course that I had overslept and kept my friend waiting. So I picked up my cell and called Vinny. He answered and seemed a bit cranky and immediately asked where I was. I was tempted to lie because I had that silly feeling of being caught that you get when you stroll into work an hour late, or your mom busts you riffling through her hamper with your nose buried in the crotch of her stockings.

I don't lie though, because honesty is the best policy (except in matters involving cross burnings, HIV status, or the age of a girl you fingered in the movie theater). Turns out that lying would have really been a blunder, as Vinny was in the hallway, outside my door. I would have felt like an ass saying I was somewhere else just to have him announce that he could hear my voice through the fucking door. I am such a bad spur-of-the-moment liar anyway, I would've blurted out some horrendously implausible explanation. ("Oh, you meant where am I now *physically?* Sorry, I misunderstood you.") So he came in and I gargled with some mouthwash so I wasn't breathing my homeless person's asshole morning breath into his face. I was still groggy with sleep and had half a boner in my sweat pants, so I really felt like a man about town.

We decided to go for coffee and chitchat a bit. To make up for my tardiness, I let him pay for the coffee and Danish so he didn't feel like a leech. An hour or so later we said our good-byes and dumb Vinny had to sit in a *wall* of Lincoln Tunnel traffic (bad accident in the tube apparently), which he never would've gotten stuck in had I woken up on time. Because I live on Forty-third Street, the traffic goes right by my building, so I could see him just sitting in his stupid truck, not moving. He was absolutely *fuming* and it pleased me to no end. Nothing worse than sitting in a massive traffic jam because of someone's lateness while you watch that person traipse away without a care in the world.

The rest of my day was pretty much a bust; I just sat around and avoided anything resembling physical activity, mindlessly fumbling with my cock while surfing the Internet.

I did three sets down at the Cellar tonight and they all went fairly well. I am trying to work on a new bit about raping the Aflac insurance duck. I had a meal after my second set and then ate apple pie à la mode. The entire time I was eating it I was just thinking of what a portly cunt with no stick-to-itiveness I am. Every time my thin lips greedily opened for more pie I visualized a shotgun entering my mouth instead.

One of my ex-girlfriends came down tonight with her friend and we hung out a bit. Seeing her is always a mix of emotions ranging from slight resentment to wanting to eat her ass until the cows come home. I tend to settle somewhere in the middle, which is being genuinely glad to see her while occasionally stealing creepy glances at her tits. We all hung outside the Cellar for a bit and then I dropped them off at a bar on the Upper East Side. I debated a prostitute on my way home, but the only streetwalker I saw was a tranny around the corner from my house. He/She/None of the Above was Mexican and about 5'5", 160 pounds. The only thing more irritating than a short, fat, foreign transsexual is a short, fat, foreign transsexual who looks like George Lopez. Maybe a wig would've helped,

I don't know. It couldn't have hurt, because this wigless idiot had hair like Tony Montana. I was afraid if I asked for a blowjob he would have leaned into my car and screamed, "Fuck the fucking Diaz brothers!"

So me and my dry, lonely dick and belly full of à la mode pie went home alone. The pillows I ordered were downstairs waiting for me so I rushed upstairs to open them and put pillowcases on them. The fact that I got excited by new pillows arriving is proof enough that my life is full of Joy, friendship, and promise.

36

JULY 19, 1968. It is hard to believe that on Monday I turned thirty-six years old. And not only is it hard to believe, it's depressing (although when people ask how old I am, I always reply, "Twenty-nine again LOLOLOLOLOLOLOL," then we chortle good-naturedly until I elbow them in throat). I really don't have much to complain about; I have now officially been sober for half of my life, I am living my dream as a comedian (I should be backhand-slapped across the face for writing that), I have friends, my health, blah blah blah. So why am I depressed half the time? Possibly because this week I signed onto Napster and downloaded two Charlie Rich songs? I was walking down Ninth Avenue yesterday and I caught myself humming "Behind Closed Doors." If I observed someone my age humming that song in public, I'd crush him against a wall with my car and consider it a mercy killing.

Rich Vos took me out for sushi tonight, a belated birthday dinner. You know, two men just eating raw fish, making eye contact, and feeding each other with chopsticks. Our waitress was a beautiful blond girl. It's odd to have a blond waitress in a sushi restaurant, so Rich asked where she was from and she said Poland. (I wonder if she thought the California rolls were actually kielbasa? HAHAHAHA, I'm incorrigible!) Of course, I wanted to ask her out on a date. Dinner later in the week, perhaps? How about a piping-hot cup of green tea, followed by nuzzling each other's anuses in Battery Park? Or maybe just a nice walk, ending with some mutual masturbation in an alley?

Unfortunately there was a mirror facing our table, so I took one sideways glance at my skull and fatty neck and chickened out. I've never seen my head look more bloated. I almost got my camera out because for a second I thought it was Jerry Lewis. I was afraid if I opened my mouth to ask for her number I would have blurted out, "Ribbit, Ribbit," and tried to eat a fly off her clit. Vos even offered to ask her out for me, which is either the sign of a good friend or a pathetic me. I turned him down, however, because the next step after that was to write her a letter asking if she likes me, including boxes with YES and NO for her to check off.

As I think more about this beautiful waitress (or as I've now come to refer to her, the Polack from that shitty sushi joint), I'm reminded of so many stories I've heard about men who have met women who at first wanted no part of them, only to change their minds and eventually get married. I don't see that happening with this girl unless she suddenly becomes a mail-order bride or victim of a white slavery ring. But how many times have you heard stories from longtime married couples of how the fellow just kept showing up and asking her out until she said yes? If you do that today they'll slap a restraining order on you. Or at the very least, one of her "guy friends" will grab you buy the scruff of your neck and scrape your teeth against the pavement.

It seems that persistence is only a charming quality in hindsight. It never ceases to amaze me how many guys have won women over by not accepting "No." We've all heard the stories: *"Well, the first time I saw your mother, I just knew I had to have her. She was out with her fiancé and his parents celebrating James Earl Ray's birthday. I kept clearing my throat and dropping motor oil cans on purpose so I could peek up her skirt. She came over and called me a creep and then stormed away. I hired a private detective to track her down. Then I showed up at her door every day with a dozen roses and a cock ring. I asked her out through the peephole week after week and in the meantime, I hired three Mexicans to beat her fiancé and his family to death with tire irons."* It's normally at this point your dopey mother schleps into the room to toss in her two cents: *"I just couldn't get over how persistent he was. At first it was showing up with roses, then it was rocks through the window and death threats over the telephone. My girlfriend kept telling me, 'Oh, just go out with him, he's cute. And he sure thinks you're the cat's meow,' and I said, 'Delores Wilkens! I will not go out with that man!' But I had to admit she was right, he sure was a handsome devil."* It's at this point your mom will giggle like the cackling, low self-esteem idiot she is because here comes the turning point in the story: *"He had such big strong arms, which went quite nicely with his naked lady tattoo and rotting teeth. I was starting to weaken and this rascal knew it. So he starts showing up every night at 2:00 a.m., drunk with a ukulele and standing in my shrubs screaming 'CUNT' until I agreed to go out with him. The very next night he came over wearing his best sharkskin suit and a tie he improvised out of a colostomy bag. We went over to Eugene's Smegma Shack for pickled pigs feet and tater fries. I tell him I want to hear 'Rock Around the Clock,' so he makes me close my eyes and fish a quarter out of his front pants pocket with my teeth. When I get up to go to the jukebox, he slips enough succinylcholine into my chocolate shake to paralyze a rhinoceros, then parks behind a Dumpster and proceeds to date-rape me with my eyes wide open. We've been together ever since."*

Were people that different back then? Or is it just me who can't tell the difference between romance and stalking? This brief synopsis can go either way: A guy has a crush on a girl but she has a boyfriend. He shyly asks her out and she says, "No, thanks." He starts leaving notes on her car and chocolates in her hallway. He sends her flowers and calls her job telling her to just give him a chance. He knows she's with the wrong guy and he won't give up . . . do you see what I mean? This story could end with, "so she finally agreed to go out with him. They went to see *The Lion King*; he cried and she fell in love. The End." But, that story, without changing any of the leadup, could just as easily end with her changing her phone number repeatedly until he finally takes a burrito shit on her windshield or attacks her with a pickax. Taking these factors into consideration, I have never been good at pursuing a woman.

So back to the important topic of the day; my birthday. Or as I say around my urban friends, "Mah birfday." It was disappointing, as most of them tend to be. I get older and never receive the gifts I want. My managers did send me two pornos and a box of latex gloves, which I intend to enjoy. I'm not too sure what the latex gloves are for, but they'll come in handy if I decide to finger my own asshole and belt out a rendition of "The Most Beautiful Girl." The pornos were fine selections, though; one of them stars Belladonna whom I *love*, and the other is about girls in Harlem licking each other's stink holes. I will watch the lesbian one first because one of the chicks in it has an extremely meaty vagina. As I've stated many times, I like a pussy that sticks out a bit. If a girl is lying on her back I want it to look like a Scooby snack. I think that's what I need in life to pick up my spirits: a girl with a great sense of humor and camel toe that's visible through a down comforter.

I am not trying to sound ungrateful when kvetching about not getting the gifts I want. It's just that people don't know me as well as I thought they did. My parents are the worst offenders. They bought me another sweater. It's the summer in Manhattan and they shop for me like I live halfway up the Khumbu Ice Fall on Mount Everest. Too bad Christmas isn't in August; I'm sure I could count on brand-new snow pants and a blowup Sherpa fuck doll. I don't know when this sweater obsession with them began. Every year I get sweaters and I don't wear them any more than I'd wear tampons or a condom. Maybe they think I'll eventually tie it loosely around my neck and waltz around like a gentleman. If I tie anything around my neck it certainly won't be a sweater (it will probably be a belt as I accidentally kill myself jerking off in the basement).

I think the worst gift I've ever gotten was from a girl I dated years ago. I drove a Mustang and she actually bought me one of those airbrushed license plates. It had palm trees on it and read JIMMY'S MUSTANG. I deserve a Golden Globe Award for smiling and thanking her instead of snapping it over my knee and gouging her fucking eye out with it. JIMMY'S MUSTANG? Are you fucking kidding me? Did she think it would keep people from vandalizing it? "Yo, man, not this one; this Mustang is Jimmy's." She probably though it would help me locate it in crowded parking lots. "Where the heck is Jimmy's Mustang? Yooo Hooo, where are you? Oh, here It Is, gang, over here!" Or maybe she was just being practical in case it was stolen. "Well, Officer, it's a black car with four wheels and some windows. However, it's unmistakably unique because it has my name and the vehicle make distinctly airbrushed onto the license plate. You'll also find AZT in the glove compartment and Gay Men's Health Crisis literature strewn about the backseat." Why JIMMY'S MUSTANG? Apparently they were out of HONK IF I'M A DOUCHEBAG bumper stickers.

Now that I think of it, she is also responsible for the second-worst gift I've ever gotten. One year for Christmas she bought me an Ozzy Osbourne clock. I've bought everything Ozzy: stickers, shirts, posters, dolls, buttons, etc. If someone had one of his logs in a baggie I'd buy the fucking thing and eat it. I am an Ozzy *fanatic* and it's miraculous that she managed to find the one piece of Ozzy paraphernalia I wanted to set on fire. But at least with her it's understandable. She was fucking me consistently, which immediately says something about her taste and judgment.

But my family? After thirty-six years they still have no idea what makes me happy. This year I really wanted a pony. There, I said it. I wanted him to be brown with a big white spot on his nose. I would name him Scraps and ride him at my birthday party while all of my friends cheered and waved balloons at me. The guest DJ would play "In Da Club" by 50 Cent and every time the line, "It's your birthday" came up, they'd all point at me and sing it. When it was time to blow out the candles, I'd get off my pony, pet his mane a bit, and then suck his cock in front of everyone. I'm not a homosexual, I just feel like it would be nice for once to give back to the pony. You know he'd be surprised. I guarantee no one's done that for him. He'd probably look down and think, "This guy's okay," and tell all of his pony friends as soon as he got back to the barn.

Someone sign this kid, he's a nut! Cat fucking in one of the infamous sweaters.

HAPPY HUMP DAY!

HUMP DAY IS common slang for Wednesday (I honestly just had to spell check "Wednesday." I always fucking spell it wrong.) and it's called that because it represents the middle of the week. Monday and Tuesday are considered the two days that are headed up, Wednesday is the tippy top, then Thursday and Friday are the downward days, sloped in such a way you can slip easily into the weekend. And as we all know, weekends are the best time to party with friends, sleep late, and fondle neighborhood children. (I am kidding, of course. I don't fondle kids; I just bounce them in my lap until a milk shake appears in my boxers.)

I was too tired to do anything on Tuesday. After waking up at 7:00 p.m. on Monday, I stayed up all night and spent the following afternoon in what felt like a haze, meandering around my apartment with half a Viagra hard-on. I did manage to get a therapeutic back rub in around eight or so before I left for work. (I say "therapeutic" because at the end of it semen blasted out of my dick so forcefully it looked as though someone attacked my comforter with a fire extinguisher.) I can't think of a more effective therapy than that, can you?

After that I wound up seeing a friend I grew up with and taking him to the Comedy Cellar. Immediately following my total bomb of a set I had a healthy chicken kebob dinner, then daintily spooned a brownie fudge sundae into my fat, reptilian face. I couldn't even enjoy it; in between every bite I had to mutter what a mushy, out-of-shape pig I am. The evening ended with me dropping my friend off at his hotel, then dragging my deep–belly buttoned torso into the elevator. I crashed for almost twelve hours and woke up this afternoon with my still-sore throat throbbing. I immediately popped an Advil and called stupid Bob Kelly to get coffee. He wasn't available, so I decided to walk to the health food store and get a fine juice. I had a shot of wheatgrass and a Veg-Out, a delightful beverage made up of carrots, beets, celery, and ginger.

I felt so invigorated I decided to race right home to sit on the toilet for thirty-five minutes and evacuate pure liquid. I always thought food had some sort of process to go through before exiting, but apparently not so with vegetable juices. Every time I drink them, my colon turns into a collapsing rain gutter. These are the types of dumps that are so devoid of any structure that you have to lift the seat when you're done and wipe underneath it because of the turd droplets that have splashed up. Nothing to bring you back down to earth like wiping the inside of your toilet when it looks like an M-80 has been dropped in it. Well, almost nothing. I'll get to that in a bit.

The rest of Wednesday was pretty uneventful. I got another shipment of DVDs, consisting of three short films I've done, all directed by Adam Dubin. *Sidesplitters* stars myself and Lewis Black (although not in that order), *American Dummy* stars Otto & George and Jim Breuer, and I get to briefly make out with Nina Hartley in the final scene. Finally, there's *The Gynecologists*. I play a man awaiting a sex change operation who gets beaten up by mobsters, one of whom is played by Rich Vos. This film is worth seeing if for no other reason then to watch stupid Vos bumble through his lines. He really does have the emotional range of the Manchurian Candidate when he acts.

I did a set at Stand Up NY in front of twelve people, which was actually a lot of fun, then struggled down at the Cellar. The audience made the judgment error of groaning and I had to discipline them with Christopher Reeve jokes and a closing bit involving Little League and incest, which is so tasteless, I'm embarrassed I wrote it. While down at the Cellar I received a call from one of my favorite Mistresses. I raced home to see her. Something else that brings you down to earth quickly is taping plastic bags to your floor because someone is coming to your home at 1:00 a.m. to use you as a toilet. You try not to think of the overall psychological implications of lying under a person as they drop logs on you.

The worst part of the whole experience, other than blocking out the idea that my grandparents are watching me from heaven and wondering what the fuck my problem is, was that yet again, the shower only had cold water. So not only was I shit on, but I had to wash away the shame and reclaim some sort of human dignity in icy-cold water.

I realize this celebration of hump day has turned into a dissertation on shit. Maybe I should change the chapter title to something more accurate like "Dump Day" or "Behaviors I Engage in Often, Including on Wednesdays."

THE BOB LEVY BENEFIT

I SPENT TONIGHT in New Brunswick at the Stress Factory performing at a benefit for Bob Levy. It was myself, Jim Florentine, Rich Vos, Eric McMahon, Artie Lange, and of course, Bob Levy. You may be wondering if Bob has cancer or has lost a limb, and the answer is no. He is getting divorced for the second time and since he has the financial planning skills of an immigrant Lotto winner, he needed money to pay the lawyers. I am very happy to help my longtime friend, but on the "good husbands list," Bob falls somewhere between Scott Peterson and Klaus Von Bulow. He drinks a lot, smokes incessantly, and closes his shows on the road by having a girl come up onstage so he can eat blue cheese out of her ass. As an issue of infidelity, this will probably be difficult to defend in court, as I doubt there are any legal precedents that allow salad dressing to be licked from the asshole of a third party. (It's common knowledge that divorce courts have historically sided with the wife in these cases. The argument that "At least there was no Worcestershire sauce lapped out of her cunt" has fallen on deaf judicial ears.) I think Bob could be an excellent husband if he lived in either Utah or Saudi Arabia.

A particularly nice surprise was that Bob's first wife showed up. They've been divorced for ten years and I hadn't seen her since. When I was first in the business, she booked some gigs and handled Bobby's career, which would explain why she's so good with tweezers (my head popped out of a *Laugh In* box as I wrote that one). She was walking through the room while Bob was on, and he looked at her and said to the crowd, "She sucked my dick." Speaking of exes, I brought my ex-girlfriend with me (from a year and a half ago, not Pumpkin) and we had a nice time together. She ran to the bathroom about twenty times and I know she wasn't doing drugs, so I assume she had the trots. She's a rare case of exes I've stayed friends with and she giggled good-naturedly when I accidentally grazed her tits forty times.

The show was completely sold out and there was a great energy in the room. Vinny Brand went on for a couple of minutes and then brought on Eric McMahon. Eric has been a friend of mine (as well as Bob and Florentine and Vos) for about fourteen years. He and Florentine used to go into New York once a week and take me with them. It was usually to the Comic Strip on Second Avenue on Monday nights. Eric is an archconservative with a tolerance level that makes John Ashcroft look like Robert Mapplethorpe. I enjoy him because he is a responsible husband and parent, yet for some reason I can still picture him digitally raping a hitchhiker.

Florentine was up next, and as soon as he hits the stage, to my delight the crowd starts yelling, "Yaaay," so he has to do Special Ed right off the bat. It's the petty little tortures suffered by your friends that make the world a brighter place. Jim told a really funny story about Bob getting blown by a stripper on the road and mentioned a couple of trains they've been on together.

After Jim it was supposed to be Rich Vos third, with Bob Levy fourth, me fifth, and Artie last. It was Vos's forty-seventh birthday (if there was more time I'd have run out to the mall and bought him a box of strawberry prostate cancer) and he wanted to go to dinner with his girlfriend. Since I am a faggot and didn't want to follow Levy (I was afraid watching his closing bit would make me yearn for a mushroom salad), Vos agreed to go fourth. Bob went up after Jim and absolutely killed; he is the only guy I know who can use "pussy farts" as a preposition.

Rich went on after him with his spray tan and washboard abs and also killed. The best part of seeing him tonight was that he brought me a sample box of three Levitras. They work rather nicely, very comparable to Viagra. The worst part of seeing him was before the show when he pulled out the photo of his cock on Levitra. I am not kidding either; Vos thought his cock looked so delicious after popping one of these pills he had to capture it on film. I won't disagree; it sure looked like quite the hiney wrecker. Carrying the photo like it's your son's graduation picture, however, was in bad taste.

I went on and did about twenty minutes of my nonsense and the response was nice. I don't really know what else to say about my own set, although it sounded like a speaker went out. The whole time I was talking it felt like I was speaking thorough a towel wrapped around the mic. After my set I went over to where my ex was sitting and debated popping a Levitra and scrapping a load on her flip-flops. It was a fleeting thought; for a moment I just felt like being a silly goose.

After I came off Artie Lange went on. This was our first time doing any sort of gig together. He's currently filming a DVD so I managed to get my dopey head into the frame a couple of times. We hung in the dressing room and trashed the FCC and liberal comics, me gaily sipping green tea and him drinking whiskey like William Holden. To anyone walking by we must have looked like Goofus and Gallant from *Highlights* magazine (bad boy Goofus is unshaven and drinking alcohol, while sweet, gentle Gallant is partaking in a green tea, hoping it's good for T-cell replenishment). So anyway, Artie had one of the best lines of the night in reference to Levy's divorce benefit: "Bob fucks some Syracuse waitress in the ass and now I'm stuck in traffic on the Jersey Turnpike." It was ninety degrees in the club so I went outside and hung with Club Soda Kenny for a bit. As the show ended Kenny helped me and Jim shamelessly whore our merchandise. All in all it was a great night; the show went well, Bob can pay his lawyers, and I got to see Rich's cock.

It's rare you get to show someone how much you appreciate all they've done for you. Levy has been a great friend since I started. He was a guy I looked up to so much early on in my career, and I will never forget our first show together. I was in the business about six months and it was my first time doing the main room at Rascals Comedy Club in Ocean Township. Bob was hosting the show, I would go on as an amateur for a few, then a headliner would close it. Bob went up and murdered and I went on and fucking *bombed*. Horribly. I will never forget; as I'm dying I actually broke character and asked the crowd, "Am I too dirty?" and some cockface in the crowd yells, "No, just get a new act," which would mean nothing to me if I heard it now, but then it was absolutely devastating. (As it turns out, it's the one time in my career I was actually heckled with good advice; my act fucking stunk to high heaven.) I told the crowd I was sorry I wasted their time and walked off stage after two minutes. As I walked, humiliated, through the crowd, some audience member said, "You'll get 'em next time," which was nice, however phonily supportive he was being. In the book of fraudulent, empty sentiments, "You'll get 'em next time" is listed as appropriate comfort for shitty comics and nine-year-old Little Leaguers.

I was beyond consolation, though; I had not only died in the big room, I had died working with a guy I really looked up to. The thing that sticks in my mind the most was the way Bob changed one of his jokes once he went back on. He used to do a joke (and a God-awful one at that) about why we go to a funeral and refer to the person as "the late John Smith." The setup to the joke was, "Has anyone here ever been to a funeral . . . besides tonight?" Then he'd launch into the punchline: " . . . Why do they always refer to the guy as the late John Smith? He wasn't late, he was at the place before you fuckin' got there." That night, after I bombed, he left out the " . . . besides tonight," line in the setup because he knew it would seem like he was referencing my bomb. I know that seems like such a minuscule, idiotic thing, but it really did move me in some odd way. I knew he was aware of how awful I felt and was trying to spare me any further humiliation. I left that gig and fucking cried the entire ride up the parkway. Anyone glancing into my car would have thought I had just suffered a miscarriage on Christmas Eve. I felt like my dream was over and that I'd finally, in my own mind, been exposed as a fraud. I wasn't funny. By the time I got home I realized that it would probably never hurt this bad again so fuck it, go up again tomorrow night. Unfortunately, the next night was when we went to war in Iraq for the first time so I had to wait a couple of days for the opportunity. And I imagine all of you amateur psychologists out there have just figured out why it is I didn't want to follow Levy tonight.

I also imagine that anyone who knows Levy would speculate that he left the line out of the setup that night because he's an alcoholic and drunkenly forgot it.

Years ago, at a wedding. Top row, from left to right: Levy; Eric McMahon and his wife, Kathy; little old me; Florentine; Vinny Brand and his wife, Vicky; Bottom row: Lenny Marcus and his friend Amy; Rich Vos; and comedian Tracy Esposito.

THE GREATEST MOMENT OF MY LIFE

IT'S ODD HOW your value system slowly changes as you grow older. Time spent with family became something to look forward to and feel grateful for, as opposed to years ago when it felt like an irritating obligation. Is it because the older I get the more human my parents become? When their hair began turning gray, did I suddenly value their company more because I finally and tangibly understood that they're growing older and are someday going to die? Or maybe I just relate to them a bit more on an eye-to-eye level now that I'm older. And things that used to mean so much have kind of lost their value a bit. Watching sports is still enjoyable but the importance of my team winning and the agony of them losing have both softened into feelings almost indistinguishable from each other. It's a saddening realization that this softening is only a pit stop on the road to indifference. It's amazing that it took until this day, in my thirty-seventh year (God, that sounds so old) to have what I will consider from here on to be the greatest moment in my life. I've never tried to choose "the best moment," although I've had my share of amazing ones: meeting Richard Pryor; talking with Sam Kinison (and getting him to autograph a napkin, which I still have); performing at Madison Square Garden and for that fifteen minutes standing alone on the same stage where Sabbath, Kiss, and Zeppelin performed. There have been some incredible moments in my life, but after today they will fast become secondary memories.

The day started out rather uneventfully; I woke up around 4:00 p.m. and popped in my contact lenses. I didn't realize that one of them was torn, so for an hour or so it felt like I had a kidney stone in my eye. I wound up sleeping so late because I didn't get to bed until around seven in the morning. After my midnight set at the Cellar last night, I stopped over at Bob Kelly's to play some cards. Bob lives on the fifth floor of my building, so it was a convenient place to socialize. Keith Robinson was there, as was Colin, Dane Cook, Bob, Matt Frost, and a comic from LA named Jay Davis. I shoveled chips and cheese and crackers and nuts into my fat face almost nonstop for three hours and in the end wound up winning a whopping sum of sixty-seven dollars. I came home and had one of my favorite working girls stop by for some late-night oral treats. She gave me head for about fifteen minutes until I shot Similac all over myself. It was an emotionally healthy ending to the day: gamble while compulsively eating shitty snack food, then pay another human being to hold my cock in her mouth like a pan flute. After she left and I had wiped the little fellers off my belly and deposited them into the toilet, I decided there was nothing else I could do to emotionally escape, so bed was probably the best option.

Bob called this afternoon, after I had woken up, and we met at Starbucks. We each had the usual: a medium iced latte with soymilk. While we were sitting outside I had the itch to gamble a bit more. Bob is also a self-hating, compulsive idiot so he of course had the itch as well. We moseyed on up to his place to play a little one-on-one Texas Hold 'Em. While Bob was converting the cash into chips I was sitting there casually picking my belly button and sniffing it. I hadn't showered yet so it was nice and ripe, just the way I like it. I always try to get people to sniff my belly button but there are very rarely any takers. Vos has a similar and equally revolting odor emanating from behind his ear. If he scrapes back there he gets an oily substance on his finger that is actually visible if he rubs it on a table. We always tell people it smells like grape jelly and then try to guilt them into smelling it by telling them that everyone else has. The disgusted faces of all of the takers send us into gales of laughter.

So anyway, today I was aimlessly digging and sniffing and I casually asked dumb Bob if he'd like a whiff. He says, "No way am I smelling that," and I figured that was the end of it. By now we'd started our poker playing. I kind of half kidding asked if he'd do it for a couple of one-dollar chips. That compulsive, greedy motherfucker said, "Two bucks? Okay." I couldn't believe my good fortune! As I said, I hadn't showered and that combined with the fact that I dumped a load into it last night/this morning really had it in tiptop, rancid form.

I took my left pointer finger (always the dipping finger of choice for some reason), and swiped it into my belly button nice and deep. I made sure I swirled it around the sides real good, leaving none of the odoriferous residue behind. This moron is sitting there with his eyes closed like he's about to do a wine tasting. I hold my finger straight and sure under his nose and watch as the look of "this is going to be slightly icky" turned into absolute revulsion. He retches a bit in the seat then gets up and bolts to the bathroom. Then the greatest moment of my life occurred: He opened the toilet lid and threw up. Oh, sweet Jesus in Heaven, thank you! I couldn't have been more satisfied if Pam Anderson's twat materialized out of thin air and fell onto my face. He kept mumbling, "Oh my God, dude," and retching and puking into the bowl. He even grabbed a bottle of Listerine because he said the smell had somehow gotten into his taste buds. I cannot express the joy of seeing this bald idiot on his hands and knees in front of the shitter losing his medium iced latte with soymilk. For those of you who are parents, take your melodramatic proclamations of the joys of childbirth and shove them up your ass. I experienced bliss in the purest sense of the word. Harmony isn't found in God or love or helping others; it's found watching an obnoxious asshole who looks like Dr. Evil vomit because the putrescent scent of your belly button has offended his system to the point of thinking it's been poisoned and needs to cleanse itself.

I was fucking *howling* while he had his gluttonous face buried in the bowl. I had my camera and snapped a picture of him. It was better than heroin. In this one moment of clarity, of purity, my whole outlook on life changed. Fuck my parents and their gray hair, fuck Richard Pryor, and fuck Madison Square Garden; someone can fill it with Doberman pinscher shit for all I care. The real meaning of life, what I've been striving for, has been hiding in my belly button all along.

This was not posed; it's an actual photo of stupid Bob puking while holding a Listerine bottle. I couldn't have been happier if the toilet lid fell down and decapitated him.

MILF

TWO HOOKERS IN three days. 7:00 a.m. on Tuesday morning I saw an ad for a girl who will give a massage with a happy ending for $100 for the half hour, and $125 for the hour. I realize this is an extremely cheap price to have a girl over but I figured, "Why not?" So I called and a girl with a very sexy voice answered and told me it is indeed her in the pictures. She was probably a four, but for those prices you can't expect Bo Derek. Unfortunately, you can expect Beau Bridges, because that is about what showed up at my door an hour later. It was the girl from the ad, but whatever magician took those photos didn't accompany her to my place. She was dumpy and awful with a backpack and bubbly personality. *Nothing* is worse than a dumpy chick who giggles a lot. The first thing she said to me was, "Can I get paid?" I guess her technique is to get the cash while the customer is still trying to figure out if she's for real of if they're caught in a *Candid Camera* gag.

She was the proverbial "real deal" so we went into my room and disrobed for the massage. As I figured, she got progressively more hideous with each article of clothing that came off; it was like watching someone slowly peel the layers off a shit onion. So I lay back naked on my bed and my cock had all the rigidity of a jellyfish tail. I had a feeling this was going to be work. She began rubbing my legs with her irritatingly small hands and then rubbed them over my stomach and up to my nipples. I normally like when my nipples are played with but her hands had all the subtlety of a gargoyle touch. As I am looking at her, something about her appearance is violating my senses and I can't figure out what it is. I suddenly realize what it is; this dumpy broad looks exactly like me. Picture my face with Michael J. Fox hair and you have this girl. She was sitting cross-legged on my bed with her tits drooping like a basset hound neck and her blubbery rolls collapsing in on each other. I almost laughed right in her fat, Uncle Festerish face. I honestly now know what it's like to be on a bed with Jim Norton naked (and to those women who claim to have cum with me during sex, your Oscars are on their way). She toyed with my cock some more but by this point it had withered like the pinky of an atrophied baby hand. Another thing that bugged me about the me that showed up was her hands had that terrible feeling hands get when they're sweaty and kind of dry; they don't rub over your skin as much as they skid like a bike tire.

When I tell you it was like looking into a mirror I am not exaggerating. She also had what looked like a Caesarean scar on the next to last roll on her belly. And don't let me forget her crotch; a bushy, horrid scene. From one angle I thought it was the Big Ragu from *Laverne & Shirley*. It wouldn't have surprised me if her cunt lips opened up and started singing "I went from rags to riches."

We did talk for a bit and she was surprisingly nice to bullshit with, I was actually enjoying her company. I couldn't really be mad at her because she was the girl from the ad, and she did have a good sense of humor. Since my cock hadn't even budged I suggested we have coffee. I told her she was too nice to act perverted with (even when a hooker shows up looking like me, I can't be mean to her) and she said, "A lot of guys tell me that." I'm sure they do. So we had coffee and I caught her looking at the clock like she was in a big hurry. It then dawned on me that she probably felt exactly the same way I did. Two silly, dumpy geese sipping coffee and wishing we were with someone who didn't look exactly like us. A few minutes later I got my happy ending: She left.

Which brings us to this morning. Around 6:30 a.m. I saw an ad for another girl who will give a hummer for $100. I called and she said she could be over in about twenty minutes. I checked out pictures of her but there were only a few odd shots of her face and tits. She was older, around forty-five and described herself as a MILF. And she was a MILF all right; a Monolith I'd Like to Forget. She rings my bell and I open the door, and she's dressed in the always sexy flannel shirt with jeans. (Nothing hotter at that hour than an older lady showing up to fuck dressed like Dan Haggerty.) We march right into my room and she kneels and goes right for the mule. The head was sopping wet and not bad at all. I suggested she take her pants off, which turned out to be a judgment error. As soon as her pants came off I could smell urine wafting up from between her awful legs (not the pleasant urine odor that we all love, but the unwashed-fat-girl-whose-been-doing-drugs-and-not-showering smell). I sit back on the bed and Ole' Alley Twat goes back to slobbering on my prick. She pushed my legs back and licked my pucker, which was relatively nice, then slid a finger over the outside. Much to my shock, five minutes later I was launching a load into her gullet. I couldn't believe that Kathy Bates had drained my nutsack in such a short period of time. I handed her the cash, she put back on her painter's clothes, then made like a banana and split. I showered immediately to remove all traces of her saliva from my testicles and doody hole, then promptly went to bed at 8:00 a.m. like a good boy.

LEGAL EAGLES

I AM WATCHING *Legal Eagles* on late-night television; it's a 1986 romantic comedy starring Robert Redford, Deborah Winger, and Darryl Hannah. Thus far, it has all the laughs of an Amish schoolhouse massacre, so I think I'll be turning it off soon. Robert Redford is a handsome guy but those three things on his face bug me to no end. I don't know what they're technically called. (Skin tags? Warts? Little face cocks?) Lemmy from Motorhead has them, but they don't irritate me on him because he's a British alcoholic, not an American sex symbol starring in a light-hearted comedic romp. As a rule, I *DETEST* romantic comedies, especially ones with rhyming titles. First of all, romance and joy are *never* funny and second, the relationships always work out in the end.

How about—just once—in a romantic comedy, you have the lead character paralyzed below the neck when he slips on a banana peel running away from the scene of a deadly arson. As he's lying in the hospital on New Year's Eve, his bubbly, smiley girlfriend (think Julia Roberts, Kate Hudson, or Andrea Yates) shows up at the hospital and as she kisses him, he can smell liquor and black cock on her breath. He calls her a trollop so she laughs and sets his toes on fire. Then her black friend from work who's "helping her grieve" comes in with his zipper open, smoking a cigar with a party hat on his head. I am torn on the casting of the coworker; he should be a very strong-willed, black-power type actor such as Yaphet Kotto or Gary Coleman. Whoever is cast must look good in fedoras, in addition to being able to tap dance while smiling brightly.

The television has been off for a while now and unfortunately I didn't get a chance to enjoy what I'm sure is a stellar performance from Darryl Hannah. I liked her a lot in *Wall Street*; she played a snotty, money-hungry socialite cunt of an interior decorator, which is probably much closer to her personality than that goody-two-shoes, cocktease of a mermaid in *Splash*. All I could think of watching that cornball flick was how much I wanted to see one of her tits accidentally torn off by the hook of a deep-sea fisherman.

Coincidentally and a bit off the subject, *Splash* is also the name of the Three Stooges–style slapstick comedy I am writing about Susan Smith. It's going to be a truly nutty film chock-full of crazy situations and fun-filled surprises. For the soundtrack I am trying to secure the rights for "Back That Ass Up" so I can dub in the word "van" over "ass." I am also trying to get one of the Wayans brothers to make a cameo, possibly as the sketch of the black car jacker she originally claimed took her children.

It may seem like I've forgotten Deborah Winger, but I only *pretended* to forget about her just to give you a panic attack. I saw about one minute of her in *Legal Eagles* and to state the obvious, she was so captivating I had a harder time tearing myself off the couch than Mabel King. The scene I saw was with her and Robert Redford, she played a lawyer and was talking into a microphone. (Darryl Hannah stood there saying nothing, much to my chagrin.) There were obviously sparks flying between Winger and Redford, and I imagine by this point in the film (I turned it off quite a while ago) they've gone to dinner and he's attempting to bonk her over the head with a law encyclopedia and rape her in the back of a station wagon.

I liked Winger very much in *An Officer and a Gentleman*, where she played opposite Richard Gere. During their sex scenes all I could think was, *What the fuck kind of awful birthmark is that on his back?* If you've seen the film you know what I mean; it looks like someone smashed a loaded baby diaper on his back; a big, shapeless brown birthmark that he better pray never becomes cancerous. Speaking of cancer, Winger was fantastic as a cancer patient in *Terms of Endearment*. I am now pausing for a moment to congratulate myself on such a fun segue. I believe this was one of her first films, if not her first, and Jack Nicholson won Best Supporting Actor for his part in it. I am hoping her character in *Legal Eagles* develops cancer and loudly blames it on radiation emanating from those stupid Frankenstein bumps on Redford's face.

I just turned the TV back on and it's Deborah Winger on *Inside the Actor's Studio*. I guess it's her night on this shitty channel. Watching her talk, I have even more respect for her acting; off screen she appears to have the personality of fly larvae. The sound of her laugh has always made me want to dip my own skull onto a buzz saw. It's a throaty, hearty guffaw with a seal-like cadence. It's horrible and if I was dating her I'd make sure to never say funny things. (I'm sure glad none of my sharp-as-a-tack comedian friends are here to zing me after that one LOL LOL ROTF LMAO.)

As I have been typing this I have been alternately eating frozen yogurt and searching on the Internet for an escort with a large clit. Not the easiest thing to find after 4:00 a.m. I wish I knew why I had such affection for vaginas that fall out like Slinkys when you pull a girl's panties aside. The bigger and meatier the better. Not only do I like meat curtains, but I prefer them to be floor to ceiling and room darkeners. I wish I didn't have this stupid fetish, it's a very hard subject to broach on the first couple of dates; "Oh, you like to water-ski . . . terrific, terrific. How about long walks in the park? You DO? HAHAHAH me too, that sounds super. Out of curiosity, when laying on your back, has your cunt ever been mistaken for a Komodo dragon's neck? Oh, no reason, just a silly curiosity. And I was also wondering if your clit bulge is visible through a spacesuit?" See what I mean? Sure, they're logical, sexy questions, but what gal is going to answer them?

When talking to a girl, I always hope she volunteers being so self-conscious about her pussy thickness that in high school she had to change for swim class facing her locker. And I hate how women don't know how completely hot this is. Some dickhead teenage boyfriend made a remark about it being too meaty or big, or he made some silly comparison between your vag and the mouth of a seventy-five-year-old pony, and you can't just let it go. I don't even mind it a little sweaty; honest Injun, I don't. As a matter of fact, I stopped into a strip club a couple of weeks ago and felt like I died and went to Meat Pussy Heaven. Jesus, there's either something in the water or every one of these chicks had their twats punched in a bar fight. It was a Utopian bevy of thick, dangling vaginas. The only one I didn't like was leaking a milky white substance out of it, which is normally the sign of a yeast infection. I am not exaggerating either, looking at her snatch reminded me of the way spittle builds up in the corner of someone's mouth when they're on antidepressants. Then again, maybe her pussy was bipolar and I'm being an insensitive ass.

Didn't matter, because the only thing less pleasant than her pussy was her breath. *God-fucking awful.* I couldn't have been more disgusted if I was blowing a homeless guy with sour milk on his dick while kneeling on shit in a monkey cage. *HORRID.* And she had teeth that looked as if they had been straightened by Jake LaMotta after a quart of vodka. Aside from that the strip club was great; I left with three fucking dollars in my pocket. I've never been jerked off in a strip club until this one, so I went home totally broke and two loads lighter. This is beginning to get silly (when I was a very little boy, my dad would call me a silly goosaballoosa). I suppose that's all I am when you think about it: a silly, fat-titted goosaballoosa, who happens to have a fetish for cunts that would be better suited on brontosauruses. Either way, I should either go to bed or put on Brubaker and jack off, pretending those things on Robert Redford's cheek are really giant clits.

THE HOLLAND TUNNEL

I HAD TO make a late night trip to my old apartment in Jersey tonight to pick up some items I'd left behind when I moved out (mainly my crayons and Beetle Bailey cock ring). I did a mediocre set at the Comedy Cellar, and since I was in the Village, logically I would leave through the Holland Tunnel, which is just a few blocks south. Since the Holland is notorious for late-night traffic, I listened to traffic reports. The total *FUCK* doing the report indicated it was smooth sailing through the Holland into Jersey. So I decided to head for it and when I did, I ran right into a massive traffic jam. This is about 1:00 a.m. and it's bumper-to-bumper and not moving. I was fucking livid. Smooth sailing? According to this piece of shit, what qualifies as bad traffic, a giant rock rolled in front of the tunnel entrance? I actually tried calling the number just to call him a cuntface. Of course, the number was busy so instead, I flung my phone against the inside of my windshield.

Obviously, I do not do well in those situations. I'm not as bad as Vos (he bites his own arm), but I do feel such rage that it frightens me. Sometimes I scream racial epithets, other times I clench and unclench my asshole while making guttural noises. My anger is just seeping out, with no real direction. I don't even know whose throat I want to cut. Is it every driver who doesn't understand the rules of multiple lanes merging into one? Or is it the boss of the Holland Tunnel for having one lane closed for construction? I realize it's an old tunnel and it needs maintenance, but what really makes me want to murder someone with a blunt object is when I am halfway through the asshole fuck tunnel and I realize it's got a lane closed so they can clean the inside of it. Why does the cocksucking tunnel need to be cleaned *every* night? When I drive by that stupid, lumbering truck that shoots water against the wall and has a big brush attached to it, I want to get out and smear donkey shit all over the windshield. Did someone actually complain that the tunnel was too dirty to drive through? They've been cleaning it for years and it always looks the same. Maybe the tunnel hierarchy will get the hint and realize that since vehicles with exhaust drive through it, dirt will accumulate, and that's okay. It doesn't need to be cleaned unless they plan on opening a fucking restaurant in the middle of it. I have never once driven through the tunnel and been upset at the sooty tiles. I don't care if there are severed baby arms hanging off the goddamn ceiling, as long as traffic is moving along nicely.

Maybe they should build a carwash at the tunnel entrance to be extra sure no dirt gets on the walls. And if they're worried about exhaust, drivers can just get out of their vehicles and put a hose from their tailpipes into their windows; this way, none of those terrible vehicle emissions will stain the inside tiles. Apparently these jerkoffs who run the Port Authority think this is the Sistine Chapel we're driving through. Or how about this: If you're hell-bent on getting the walls clean, make prisoners stand with their faces against the walls and clean the filthy tiles with their tongues. This way both lanes can be kept open and I won't have to drip piss all over my jeans because I've been in traffic for forty minutes whizzing into a Starbucks cup.

And if there are ten lanes going into the tunnel, why aren't at least eight of them E-ZPass? Why the fuck should I have to sit in traffic leading up to the tolls because some weekend warrior Jersey prick likes to fork over cash instead of just having it deducted from a monthly account? Some people are paranoid the government is going to track them. Are these fuckheads for real? They think they're so critical to national security that the government is going to track their plates to see how many times they go into Manhattan on the weekend. *No one gives a shit about your driving habits, assholes.* For the record: If you drive more than four miles a month and don't have E-ZPass, your legs should be crushed in a forklift accident. Get with the times, motherfucker.

Another reason the cash lanes are still there is because the irritating union is making sure that at least a few cranky, douchebag toll collectors are working at any given time. Fucking miserable, humorless shitbags. That's the best part of E-ZPass: It's not even the time you save, it's the fact that you can now avoid looking at their outstretched hands and stupid "a chimp-can-do-my-job" faces. I used to *HATE* when I'd give one of these overpaid, time-and-a half asshats my money, ask for my receipt and say, "Thank you," and they wouldn't even look over, much less acknowledge me with a "You're welcome." My dick used to throb fantasizing about pointing a shotgun at their rude, indifferent profiles and blasting their brains all over the inside of the booth. I do realize they deal with people all day; I am not expecting confetti or a hand job with my toll payment, just normal, decent, human courtesy from these soon-to-be-extinct piss buckets. I am so glad they're being replaced by a cigarette pack–size sensor on the insides of our windshields. I love it. In fifty years their uniforms will be hanging in museums and we'll be telling our grandchildren, "When I was your age, I couldn't just go directly into the tunnel; I had to stop and hand over cash to a moody primate." The little lad will giggle with delight and disbelief, so just to drive home the point you'll have to plant your fist in his naïve little face right there in the middle of the museum.

THE DUMP WHISPERER

IT'S A RAINY night tonight in New York. Had five sets and like a scatterbrained little cuddle monster, I left my umbrella at home. I took it out of my closet before I left, then stopped in the mirror to practice some break-dance moves. Sometimes I'll take off my shirt, put clamps on my meat tits, and pop lock for hours. I lost myself in the music and moonwalked out the door sans umbrella. So I stopped in the store to pick one up and I actually found myself looking for a masculine color. Odd how such idiotic things are attributed to masculinity and femininity. I really liked the lime green umbrella and grabbed it, then suddenly had visions of white supremacists beating me with it screaming, "Faggot with a girl's umbrella!! Faggot with a girl's umbrella!!" so I put it back and grabbed the blue one. Black would have been the manliest choice, I suppose, but the blue one was just so pretty. I could see myself holding flowers in one hand and my blue umbrella in the other, gracefully traipsing about the Big Apple, getting to know people. They'd say hello, possibly even whistle. I'd giggle and give a coy smile. I'd also love to purchase a large hat of some sort to match my umbrella, like the kind Sandy Duncan wore in *Roots*. I am very much looking forward to the next rainy day so I can be seen all over town in my smart new outfit.

Tonight's shows went relatively well as I am working on my new, funny stage persona, which involves me doing cartoon voices and tooting a bicycle horn after every punchline. I met a girl at the late show who would pass for fuckable if I drank a quart of gin and then bathed my apartment in ultraviolet light. We both enjoyed a couple of breath-freshening

Middle-Eastern lamb kebobs; then I brought her back to my pad to play a little "hide the mushroom in the baby maker." As soon as we walked through the front door, she asked to use the bathroom. Once inside I heard the water turn on immediately, which meant one of three things: She was washing her meat curtains, was tinkling and needed the water to motivate her, or was taking a shit and using the water to mask the gurgling stomach grumbles and log splashes in the bowl. Ten minutes later she walked out of the can and did a telltale thing: She closed the door quickly behind her. I've pulled this stunt many times myself at girls' houses, not wanting the dumpsterlike odor to waft out and belt her in the sinuses.

Unfortunately I had to tinkle, so as soon as she walked out, I walked in and my worst fears were confirmed. There's nothing more enchanting than preparing to fuck a girl right after she's dropped a Manwich-sized dump in your bathroom. She must have been embarrassed when she realized I was walking in right after her. I know I would have been. I tried not to make an issue out of it, but I'm pretty sure she knew I got a good whiff by my loud coughing, followed by walking back into the living room with a clothespin on my nose. The sex was uneventful and not worth going into (from her point of view, I mean).

CURRENTLY IN BRAZIL

I AM SITTING here in the business center of my hotel in Rio. So far I am having a stellar time. I am psyched because we're going to one of the local whorehouses tonight. The brothels here really are amazing. You walk in and get a locker, then change into a robe and proceed upstairs into the dance club wearing nothing but your robe and a pair of flip-flops (which dig into my toes horribly, I *loathe* flip-flops). Once you're upstairs you sit in a bar/lounge area that has about twenty-five girls dancing in bikinis. This is not like an American strip club either, no snotty girls trying to give you a shitty, no-contact lap dance for thirty bucks while they stare vacantly off into space. None of those cornball stripper moves; the face rubbed barely against the crotch accompanied by a hair flip, or that awful one where they put their ass kind of near your face and give one of their cheeks a slap; ooohh, so naughty she had to discipline herself! Fucking idiots. I'd be more turned on watching someone spank a baby seal with a canoe oar. Nothing worse than an entitled, no-contact cocktease. You know the rules: She bends over in front of you, and if you *dare* to touch her shitter, some ex con bouncer will grab you by the pubes and toss you through the classy neon window.

The Brazilian establishments have music playing, of course, and it's every bit as horrid and unlistenable as the music in American strip clubs. You sit down and girls start coming up to you fairly quickly. And these girls are extraordinarily hot (and dirt poor, which is always a plus). Sometimes they'll ask you for a drink, so you give her your numbered bracelet (there is *no cash exchanged with the girls*, it's all done downstairs at the end). And because of this arrangement, there is no haggling over prices. Forty-minute and one-hour sessions are available, and every girl gets the same rate. A bit like communism when you think about it.

If you and the gal hit it off, she'll sit down and start making out with you. *"You make out with hookers in a brothel??"* You're darn tootin' I do! As long as she doesn't have bleach breath and a foamy white beard on her chin, it's all roses to me. Once you go upstairs, anything that's okay with the girl is okay to do. Some love to make out, some do it but only reluctantly. Some love to be fucked in the ass, others have to be cajoled with a fifty you snuck up in your robe pocket. Since there's a language barrier, occasionally there are communication breakdowns. However, pushing your helmet against a girl's brown eye is fairly international for, "Come on, let me stick this where the sun don't shine, you silly goose." Still others are very quiet, while some prefer to babble in Portuguese until you either cum or take a foreign language class to figure out if she's insulting you.

Another thing I've noticed is that there is very little attitude between the men in the room. I suppose it's because all you have to do is nod at a girl and you can fuck her, so there really isn't much cause for a guy to think he's anything other than a dopey John. This also means that we're all guaranteed to get laid. Why cause a big to-do when there's a load just waiting to be shared with a special someone? Another reason could be that we're all wearing robes and flip-flops, and no one wants to be punched in the jaw and then have their cock bobble out as they tumble backward into a prostitute (especially if you have a Viagra hard-on at the time—it will appear that you're enjoying your beating at the hands of the other gentleman). The biggest reason, though, is that *no one* wants to wind up in a Brazilian jail. One minute you're on vacation having some good-natured fun and the next minute you're in a jujitsu hold with a pair of real man's balls on your nose.

As of this writing I've fucked eleven different girls in four days, and every one of them would've spit their gum at my nose back home in New York. *"He has to go to another country just to fuck hot girls for money? How pathetic."* He does, and he is.

I'D LOVE TO LIVE IN RIO

WHERE TO BEGIN? I suppose I can start with my horrible intestinal cramps. For the last twenty-four hours or so it's felt like someone is reaching inside of my stomach and squeezing my lower intestines, relaxing for thirty seconds, then squeezing again (very similar to the method an older gentleman may use when reaching into the shorts of a youngster to make sure he isn't hiding any stolen candy). The cramps started yesterday morning and had me panicking because my flight home was at 7:00 p.m. When you're on a plane, the only thing worse than sitting next to an Arab with a wick sticking out of his shoe is having stomach problems. The night before was our last full night in Rio, so of course I ate like a fat hog because that's what I'd been doing every night. I dumped a shitload of garlic bread into my greedy face, which naturally made my mouth dry later in the evening. To quench my thirst I gave in and drank tap water from the hotel faucet, which I now believe was the source of my trouble. Who'd have imagined that tap water from a Third World country could give you stomach discomfort? I really am a dummy. Maybe next year I can do something healthier, like taking a trip to Calcutta and only drinking fluids bottled directly from the catheters of malaria patients.

The trip itself was very relaxing and enjoyable. We stayed at a hotel about ten minutes from all of the action. The first two times we went we stayed at the Rio Othon Palace, which is literally a block from the main nightclub, Help. This is a club very much like the ones here in the States, except that every single girl in there is a prostitute. And I do

With Patrice in a whorehouse locker room. You can tell we're preparing to leave by the shame sweat coating his face.

mean *every last girl*. You can have anyone you want just by walking up to them. I finally know what it's like to be good-looking. "Hi, how are you? My name? Oh, it's Jim, what's yours?" Then twenty minutes later you're back in your hotel room throat-fucking her bareback while praying she's HIV negative. The reason we didn't want to stay that close to the action is because realistically speaking, Brazil is a dangerous country in certain places. We didn't like the idea of people being able to watch us walk to and from the hotel at all hours of the night; better to just hop in a cab when you leave the club. Even hopping in a cab can be a problem because the police have checkpoints along some of the roads. The cops sit there like leopard seals while we shuffle along like a bunch of idiotic, quacking penguins with razor-toting prostitutes in tow. They pull your cab over; you get out and are searched. There is always the chance of being set up on some bullshit drug charge just so they can shake you down. I always refuse to take a cab with any of the girls; I make them take a separate one behind me. This way the cops won't see us together and even if my cab does get pulled over, there's no chance of her tossing a bag of something on the floor and getting me arrested. I'm amazed at the risks I take just to consort with whores. For those of you who have never been to Brazil, it kind of feels like *Pretty Woman* meets *Midnight Express*.

I fucked quite a few different girls this week. But it wouldn't be a truly Jim Norton vacation if I hadn't been stood up. And I was—twice. Two different Brazilian prostitutes promised to show up at my hotel on two different nights and never did. Do you have any idea what it does to your self-esteem when women don't even want to suck your cock to pay the rent?

Of course I didn't go to Brazil alone; that would be way too creepy. Vacationing with friends is fine, but if you fly more than nine hours all alone just to get blown, you probably need psychiatric help. I was accompanied by Jason Steinberg, Bob Kelly, Patrice Oneal, and a comedian I'd never met named Larry.

Standing in the lobby, waiting for a hooker who never showed up.

LARRY

The first time I met him was this week in Rio. Bob and I flew in and met Patrice and Jason at an outdoor café where the whores tend to stand around and mingle. It really does make for a fine dining experience. Nothing whets my appetite like a desperate, drug-starved girl with a fat pussy bulge and scars on her legs. Larry was sitting with those two when Bob and I strolled up. He is a relatively quiet guy who kind of resembles Snoop Dogg in the lower part of his face. I would be happy to comment on the upper part of his face if I'd ever seen it, but he wears sunglasses and a tilted baseball cap every waking moment. The only time I saw him not grinding up against someone was when he was eating. I really loved this guy; *EVERY* time I saw him he was making out with a girl. These are Brazilian street hookers, and Larry was acting like Michael Corleone on his wedding night. You never saw a more passionate guy; it wasn't just kissing, but the loving, hold-the-face kisses you give that special someone. And he didn't discriminate—he made out with gorgeous girls as well as one chick who I think played offensive line for the Steelers, and another who looked like a fat Cicely Tyson. (I almost had to do an intervention on that one. The guys from *Jackass* wouldn't have been caught fucking this girl.) And don't get me wrong, he is a good-looking guy with a strapping, manly build; the type of arms that could really hold a fellow down, if you know what I mean.

One problem is that it's very common to come back with a cold of some sort from Brazil; all of that kissing doesn't go unpunished. I believe they call it "the crud." Larry did have one moment like that at dinner, a brief panic as he tried to fight a cough and had liquidy snot tobogganing out of his nose. But that didn't deter him. Shit, it didn't even slow him down because he got caught up in the matrix of Rio, as most of us do. If it moved, he gently held it by the face and gave it tender kisses. For the first few days he's back in America, I'm sure he'll instinctively try the same shit and get kneed in the nuts.

BOB AND JASON

It's no accident that I'm lumping these two idiots together. They pulled off the impossible: They spent a week in Rio and didn't get any prostitutes. And I do mean not a one. Neither one of them is into paying for sex. I had been to Brazil with both of them before so I knew the deal, I just don't fucking get it. How do you not want to hand over cash to a girl so she'll slobber on your cock like a quadriplegic playing the harmonica? When I think about this I'm not sure whether to admire them or throw up on them. The hotel we stayed at had three pools, tennis courts, and a basketball court and they were perfectly content to occupy most of their time with these shitty, mundane activities. Truly mind-boggling.

Jason is a comedy manager and handles Patrice as well as Rich Vos and a bunch of other comics. He does most of the hotel planning and things of that nature, as he is pretty organized, as well as being one of the most notoriously cheap fuckers cast of Los Angeles. He gets money knocked off everything including our hotel rooms (he got me upgraded to a suite for no extra cash) and meals. He whips out this travel agent card wherever we go and usually gets a discount (although some places stare at it like he's just pulled a cancerous liver out of his wallet and politely tell him to fuck off and pay up). I was hoping he'd yank that stupid card out and hand it to a hooker. He's a guy I like a lot and I'm not speaking about him behind his back; it's just a fact. Some things in life just are; I like to be pissed on, Patrice is fat, Jason is cheap.

For a long time Bobby resembled a Puerto Rican kid-toucher, until he shaved all his hair off. Now he just looks like Donald Pleasance. Bob was happy to just get away and hang with his friends and fill his emotional void with food. He ate fairly healthy the whole trip, although if he mentions that irritating South Beach Diet one more time I'm going to dip a nightstick in carbohydrates and rape him with it.

One afternoon I was at the tennis court watching him and Jason bat the ball back and forth and I asked if I could grab a racket and play a bit. Bob is a competitive psychopath and refused to give it up, screaming that he and Jason were having a tournament of some sort. Bald and shirtless, he resembled a graceless, lumbering otter. I just want to get a few swings in and this cocksucker acts like he's Andre Agassi. He was right not to give up the racket though, because once he did, every ball Jason lobbed to me I tried to smack over the fence and into the ocean so that cheapskate would have to pay for them. I think they both had a great time; Bobby eating and Jason haggling. And at least they both flew home with their genitals intact.

DR. DILDO

From this day forth, Patrice Oneal is only to be referred to as Dr. Dildo. I thought I knew what sexual addiction was until I spent another week in Rio with this dysfunctional sociopath. First of all, he had to go down almost a week before the rest of us because apparently eight days of paying for pussy is not quite sufficient. He has earned his new nickname because he did not travel to Brazil emptyhanded; no, he traveled with a duffel bag full of dildos. And these weren't normal dildos, of course; that would be almost understandable. These were made of glass. Some people like glass dolphins, some prefer glass unicorns, and now I realize there are those who only like glass objects shaped like giant cocks. In addition to being shaped like cocks, they had ridges on them. I wanted to stand one up straight and watch a daredevil attempt to climb it.

To prevent such precious items from chipping (and undoubtedly causing twat-nicks not unlike the ones I get shaving my face), each dildo is individually stored in a velvet pouch. And in addition to the multicolored, different-size dildos, there were of course two vibrators. One was fairly normal looking and only about a foot and a half in length, the other looked like the Seattle space needle with a rounded top. He brought all of these things just to make Brazilian prostitutes orgasm (and in the process avoid any meaningful human contact). Every time we left the hotel to go to the brothel, this jackass was lugging an Adidas bag full of sex toys. He'd bring it into the whorehouse and leave it in his locker. Whenever he wanted to take a girl into a private room, he'd have to go back down the elevator, reopen his locker, get the forty-pound bag of shame, and head back up. That must have been a real treat for the hookers: to see a 6'4", 300-pound black gentleman mosey into the room wearing a short robe carrying a clanking sack of glass phalluses.

One night Patrice agreed to let me watch him work his magic on one of the girls back in the hotel. I was a bit pessimistic at first; seeing the girl lay back while he casually plugged in the vibrator had all the sexual tension of Olivier's scenes in *The Marathon Man*. I was half expecting him to ask, "Is it safe?" and then knock her teeth out with a pair of Ben Wa balls. The girl was a bit nervous and in hindsight, I can't blame her. Here a giant goon is about to insert electrical equipment into her snatch while I knelt there staring between her legs and blinking rapidly.

The other bit of loveliness I forgot to mention is the bottle of Eros lubricant he brought, which was approximately the size of a grain silo. He started off by pouring lube onto her vagina, then turned the vibrator on. I am not sure what setting he started it on but I am pretty sure this thing had a clutch on it. She was giggling at first as he applied it to her clit. After a couple of moments of soothing talk from him (or what passed for soothing talk; all I saw was a creep patting a pretty girl's stomach while repeating,

"Calmo, calmo,") she stopped giggling and began to relax. He then picked up glass dildo #435 and worked it slowly inside of her. The amazing thing was watching her try to resist. She wanted to fake it; she didn't want to really give in and cum. Well, life is what happens when you're making other plans; she came all right, and came hard. To watch her lose the battle and feel good for real was intense. And she wasn't faking; there was a wet spot on the bed the size of the Elephant Man's head. I was truly in awe and vowed to refer to this special man as Dr. Dildo from that day forth.

I may have left some things out but please forgive me; it's late, I'm tired and if I attempt to fart right now an Oompa Loompa will have to show up and clean out my boxers.

A moment of quiet reflection with the good doctor.

TOUGH CROWD

I'M HEADED TO Sacramento for a gig and am currently sitting in Houston at the tail end of a fifty-minute layover. I've just boarded the plane and as habit dictates, I am sipping a tomato juice with lime. The only time I ever even consider sipping tomato juice is on an airplane. I don't know why, but somehow it just feels gentlemanly. To look at me sipping, you'd think I never duct-taped garbage bags to my bathroom floor and yelled, "Bombs away!" as a dominatrix fired logs onto my chest with the precision of an F-16. At the moment, there is a woman coughing behind me and I'm fighting the urge to smash her gums with the heel of my Doc Marten. I just got over a sore throat and now this bitch is going to give me small pox because she can't cover her goddamn mouth when she coughs.

We are now about two hours into the flight. I had to shut down my computer for takeoff, then I read some of my new book (a science fiction novel about a slave who flees the south by learning to fly called *Cut the Malarky, Bub)*. I dozed off for a couple of hours, but slept poorly due to the hacking broad behind me, who I hope dies in her seat. To listen to this asshole, you'd think she spent the last twenty years snacking on Pall-Malls and asbestos. I'm sitting in first class due to a mileage upgrade, and trying hard not to let her whooping cough wreck my fancy experience. I am also trying to peek up the dress of a woman who is squatting down in the aisle riffling through her bag. I wish she were thirty years younger; I'd bribe her with lemonade to do a summersault.

I woke up a few minutes ago to the smell of baking chocolate chip cookies. There is *no* smell on earth better than that, save new leather, my belly button, and asparagus piss. So the flight attendant, a large, burly fellow with a goatee, walks down the aisle and gives everyone a cup of water. I recognize this is a prelude to the cookie and begin to salivate. I only take one gingerly sip of the water so I can use the rest to wash down my yummy chocolate chip treat. After distributing the water, he comes out carrying a tray of cookies and I have to restrain myself from yelling, "Yaaaay," and clapping wildly like a retard. It's not that I'm embarrassed about my unbridled joy over the cookie, it's just that clapping wildly makes my blubbery tits jiggle and I don't need to be reminded of that right before I eat such a fattening dessert.

So he goes to the first row, then the second. Then this *motherfucker* proceeds to skip my row and give cookies to the row behind me. He blatantly passed over my row. I sat there hurt and humiliated; images of Fredo and fat girls and Susan Lucci and everyone else who's ever been stepped over and ignored flashed through my mind. I figured this must be some mistake, so every time he walked by I looked up eagerly and tried to make eye contact, hoping he'd see my hurt face and come rushing over with a cookie, perhaps two. No such luck. This horrible, soulless cocksucker had forgotten about me. I briefly entertained the idea of writing to Continental Airlines, but even in my desperate state I realized that any post-9/11 letter of concern written to an airline revolving around cookie distribution would seem trite. I decided to take matters into my own hands and call the flight attendant over to ask for it myself. Complete shame engulfed me as he stopped at my row and I looked up and meekly stated, "Sir, I didn't get my chocolate chip cookie." Being a professional, he apologized and fetched me one. He was outwardly pleasant about it, but the steely, disgusted look in his eyes implied he wanted to throw the cookie into my piggish gullet and then offer me a mouthful of ball juice to wash it down with.

I have two shows tonight and normally I hate flying on the day of a show, but I had no choice. Last night was the final episode of *Tough Crowd* and I obviously had to be in New York for it. The final show guests were myself, Keith, Nick, Patrice, and Greg, and it was monumentally depressing. We all knew it was coming to an end long before the official announcement, so while we are disappointed, none of us were surprised. I never felt like the network loved us; we got very little promotion and when we did, it seemed to be promotion that didn't accurately reflect the show. Colin used to go nuts over dick jokes being used in the promos, because while he felt they had a place on the show, he hated it being sold that way and he was correct.

Janeane Garofalo hating my guts on our first episode.

The most frustrating part of the cancellation is that it's very rare you find a gig you enjoy as much as we did this one. We are all friends, which is why many of the episodes degenerated into us straying from the topics and just shitting all over each other. We're also extraordinarily comfortable with each other, and from that comfort level comes very honest interactions. Every one of us was aware that if you came to the table with some phony applause-generating horseshit you were going to be called out and shredded by the other comics. Not that we never did it, but we weren't surprised when our assholes got ripped out for it when we did.

Three months after *Opie & Anthony's* cancellation in 2002 (everywhere I go this seems to happen; maybe I'm the fucking problem), we began formulating *Tough Crowd*. The show quickly went from a diversion from my depression to a part of my career that I loved. I forget who named the show (I think it was DiPaolo), but we all came up with different ideas, most of which were fucking hideous. One of the suggestions I submitted, and I am truly embarrassed by it, was *Quinntessential Colin* (you know, because his last name is *QUINN*; get it?). We really had no idea what the show would wind up looking like, just a rough idea about the structure. Keith Robinson and I shared an office and I can't tell you how many times Colin walked in and found us both sleeping, our feet up on our respective desks. He was trying to get a show picked up and two of his alleged writers were napping on the clock without a care in the world. I never felt guilty, though; he should have known better than to hire us (especially Keith, who is black).

Looking like a nervous, itchy fatso sharing a laugh with Seinfeld.

My biggest fear in doing the final episode was that I was going to start blubbering and make a horrid spectacle of myself (FACE SLAP: "You can act like a man!"). At one point it looked like Giraldo was going to cry and there was a period where Patrice was going to weep (and I quote Colonel Kurtz) *"like some . . . grandmother."* I think we all realized in the greenroom how much we were going to miss this show; we would normally start trouncing each other and the topics the minute we walked in. If it wasn't Nick complaining about the dykes running show business, it was Patrice being an obnoxious asshole and bothering people who worked for the show, or Keith *Sssssssshhhhing* anyone who happened to be in the dressing room regardless of what they were talking about or how uncomfortable his shushing was making them.

I always enjoyed getting people who were new to the show to start talking, then *slamming* the dressing-room door hard while they were mid-sentence. It really pissed some people off (Jeff Garland was irritated, to say the least, and Hal Sparks *despised* me for it). Stephen Colbert laughed loudly when I slammed the door in the middle of some awful story he was telling, but I didn't have the balls to do it to Jon Stewart or Paul Mooney.

Colin would pop in a lot, say something vicious and cutting, then about-face on his awful, cancer patient legs and traipse down the hall to his dressing room before you had a chance to respond. I had a lot of huge laughs with these guys, which shouldn't be surprising; they're some of the funniest people in the country. I'll still see them on a regular basis at the Cellar and I'm sure we'll continue to abuse each other, but it was nice being able to do it on television. And while I am irritated with Comedy Central's dumb decision to cancel the show, I can't sit here and trash them, either. The reality is they did put us on the air for two years and gave us a great special (*Tough Crowd Stands Up*). My only real hope is that we're not replaced with a cartoon or British homosexual.

Sitting on Saddam's toilets in his Baghdad palace.

I loved the fact that at Colin's insistence we left things in even when they bombed, because it's honest. Comedy is not always a perfectly timed smooth gem, and it certainly doesn't always elicit the hoped-for response. Sometimes comedy is sloppy and poorly delivered and falls facefirst in the toilet. He refused to be some polished, blazer-wearing sap of a host and crucified any one of us when we tried to lapse into that smooth, disingenuous nonsense.

You saw us as we really are on *Tough Crowd*—sometimes very funny, other times embarrassingly unfunny, sometimes hypocritically self-righteous and preachy and other times just plain mean. *Tough Crowd* absolutely made me a better comedian because it forced me to write consistently about things I probably wouldn't have written about otherwise, as well as forcing me to look at my own idiocy and periodic phoniness. The show was definitely not perfect; we talked all over each other, were sometimes too jokey, occasionally we indefensibly sucked. But we were always honest. Not just with one another but with the viewers; we never tried to lose our flaws just to make you like us. I always loved how Colin would expose these flaws in all of our individual relationships. There were dummies who thought that was "too inside," but I think that people related to the honesty behind the assessments; our friendships are really no different than anyone else's. And also, the more these flaws were talked about and made fun of, the more the public got to know us: Nick is mean, Patrice is loud, Greg is smart, Keith is stupid, and I'm a pervert. Nick will undoubtedly be irritated that I called him mean and Greg smart, and Keith will somehow manage to find pride in being called stupid.

It's one of the best things I've done in my career, and on some level, I'll always miss it.

One of the greatest moments of my life. Not only did I get to do *Tough Crowd* with Carlin, at the last minute Colin added me to the third act sketch the two of them were doing. They played priests and I waltzed in in the middle of it all dressed like an altar boy, handed Carlin an album, and asked him to sign it. Colin informed George I am a big fan of the seven words you can't say on television. Carlin informed us he has an updated version of the seven words you can't say on television: "Welcome to The Jim Norton Show, everybody!" He then calls us cocksucking motherfuckers and walks off screen. I was in heaven. Thanks, Col.

COUCH POTATER

THERE WAS A story recently about a five-hundred-pound woman who laid on her couch so long her skin became grafted to it. I read today that she was 4'10", which is approximately forty-five feet shorter than she should be to maintain that weight. Her height-to-weight ratio would only be considered healthy if she were made of lead and lived on Jupiter. She was having trouble breathing one night and her quick-thinking husband called the paramedics. That monster is lucky I wasn't married to her, or the call would have been slightly less compassionate:

"911, what's your emergency?"

"My wife can't breathe."

"Is something blocking her airways, sir?"

"Yes, the piece of electrical cord I wrapped around her fat neck."

"Can you repeat that please, sir?"

"You heard me, toots. I have one foot on her face, the other on her butt, and I'm pulling on it so hard, I just shit into my socks."

"Sir, can you sit her in the upright position?"

"That's a negative. The last time she sat up was in Feb of '98. UPS delivered a large box and she bolted upright in a panic, thinking it was exercise equipment. Turns out it was just a pair of pants she ordered from a clothing wholesaler in Indiana who specializes in making casual slacks for wooly mammoths."

"Sir, I understand you're upset but it's imperative you adjust her to be in the sitting position."

"I'd love to oblige, but you see, her being unable to sit up is part of the problem. One night after polishing off an elk for dinner she said she had a headache and wanted to lie down. So she stretches out on the couch and hasn't been up since. That was six years ago. And the excuses are endless; everything from, 'I'll try tomorrow, two horseflies were fucking on the bridge of my nose and swatting at them really tuckered me out,' to '*American Idol* is starting, I'll get up as soon as the season is over.'"

"I'll send the paramedics immediately, sir. What's your address?"

"She's been lying here so goddamned long her skin has grafted itself to the couch. Paramedics won't do any good, send an upholsterer."

"I'm sorry, sir, did you say she grafted herself to the couch?"

"Yes, ma'am, just like a fucking comic book character. Stan Lee couldn't have come up with something this awful if he stuck Mama Cass in a laboratory with a sofa and exposed them both to gamma radiation. And the worst part is she's sitting on the remote. I've had six years of the Home Shopping Network and I can't take it anymore. I own 3,700 gold-plated hoop earrings, forty Ben Franklin commemorative toilet seat covers, and more than 45,000 baseball cards worth a grand total of eleven dollars, minus shipping and storage. We had the presidential dish collection but she got hungry and ate all the ones up to Eisenhower."

"Try to remain calm. We've traced the call and help is on the way."

"Help?? Where the hell were you six years ago? You don't seem to understand how embarrassing it is to invite your buddies over to watch the ball game and have to explain why you all have to sit on the floor because your couch is occupied by a giant sea tortoise who may or may not shit into a frying pan."

"I do understand, sir, but . . ."

"It's kind of the ultimate in irony. She's taking a dump on our living-room furniture and still yelling at the kids to get their dirty feet off the table."

"Are there young children in the house, sir?"

"Nah, not that young. We stopped fucking almost four years ago; I was afraid if I knocked her up, she'd give birth to an ottoman."

"The ambulance is almost there, sir. I need you to remain calm and not get agitated."

"Aww heck, maybe it's my fault, too. The first two years of her couch occupation was just kind of a running joke, we had fun with it. We'd play hide-and-seek and I'd pretend not to know where she was. And every year around Christmas we'd drape lights all over her and get our pictures in the local paper. I started to get concerned when our pets began disappearing and by the end of the third year, I was plum disgusted and I think she could sense it. To keep my pitching arm in shape I'd stand ten feet away, wind up, and fire Ho Hos and Ding Dongs into her mouth. Sometimes, I'd come home from work and tell her what block I was on when I started to smell her. Nothing got her moving. I knew all hope was lost in 2002 when I ran in screaming, *'FIRE!'* and instead of trying to get up, she asked for marshmallows and a stick."

"Just hang tight, sir, they're pulling up to your house now."

"No need to; she's dead. You better get back on that radio and tell the boys to bring wall-cutting saws, a flatbed truck, and a can of Lysol the size of the Chrysler Building. And when the police show up, I'll just put on a bright orange hat and tell them it was a hunting accident. Now maybe I can finally take all the money I was spending on her food and get a few things I need, like new sneakers and a Lamborghini."

In actuality, the police and fireman spent hours trying to pry this monstrosity off the couch and were unable to. As you may have surmised because of my glib allusion to it, she did in fact die. How did you think this story ended? With a chipper smile and a celery stick? Grow the fuck up already.

THE VOYEUR BUS

I'D HAVE TO say the thing that really cemented me as a regular guest on the *Opie & Anthony* show was the Voyeur Bus incident. Up until that time I had been stopping in and periodically reporting on my prostitute addiction and firing out AIDS jokes whether they fit the situation or not. On this particular day, there was a group of hot girls preparing to get on a private bus with extra large windows so they could ride around Manhattan and flash their tits at passersby.

I didn't know the guys who were in charge of the bus, but they reminded me of child pornographers, minus the integrity and good humor. Lewis Black was also in studio. Opie asked me if I wanted to take the bus ride and act as a correspondent, calling the show to give location updates and anything else I felt would be pertinent. It was a tough decision, but I finally decided to board the bus filled with half-naked teenagers. I felt that if I was going to be a team player, I'd have to make such sacrifices. In the meantime, I had also talked Lewis Black into going with us. At first he said no, until I leaned in and said, "You fucking idiot, they're all topless teenage chicks. What else do you have to do today?" He responded by wagging his finger rapidly and agreeing with me. Also on the bus were on-air personality Psycho Mark, producer Rick Delgado, and Steve C., who ran the website and did production work.

So we began our trip around Manhattan at about 3:30 that Thursday afternoon, sent off by Op, Ant, and a couple of hundred potential rapists in WOW T-shirts. As the bus began rolling, these lunatics were following it on the sidewalk and screaming at the girls. The girls, by the way, were lovely. I don't remember their names or anything about them above the shoulders or below the torso. Except for Melanie. She was about nineteen, very talkative, and had a round, plump hiney. It was the main motivation in getting me on the bus. That and she had those really dark, Hershey Kisses nipples. I *LOVE* those. The type of areolas that start at the nipple and end somewhere near the third rib. I don't know why but that makes me salivate.

So we started the trip and everyone's spirits were high; the girls were giggling and flashing out the window, Lewis was staring with his mouth open, Rick was already calling in, and I was leaking enough pre-cum to lubricate a Slip 'N Slide. As the jocularity ensued, the only bit of discomfort I experienced, other than repressing the desire to commit sodomy, was wanting a cigarette. And I was shit out of luck because the bus was nonsmoking. Lewis was also feeling it ten minutes into the trip. Little did we know, but those butts we choked down outside before getting onto the bus would be the only ones we'd have for the next thirty hours (insert dramatic organ music).

To describe the trip moment by moment would be redundantly tedious because there are only so many ways to write "She flashed her tits, guys outside the bus screamed, Rick fixed his hair, and I squeezed my shaft so hard I almost blacked out." We did, however, attract quite a bit of attention. It was December and the streets were packed with holiday shoppers. We even had a cop driving by the side of the bus, keeping people from hitting the windows, and enjoying the view himself (and collecting evidence, as we later found out). There isn't much to say about the non-*O&A* guys on the bus; I didn't really get to know them. They were lecherous creeps with that awful three-day stubble growth beard and, I imagine, very low-level porn connections. ("Dude, my cousin has a friend who takes freelance pictures for *Swank* magazine." That type of shit.)

As we went down past City Hall, a CNN reporter hopped on the bus with us. Apparently this vehicle full of juicy-titted success stories was developing quite the little reputation. The reporter interviewed the girls and I think I tried unsuccessfully to get my slug-shaped skull into the story. They talked to Lewis as well, who was the only one of us with a real career at that point. They were surprised to see such a bright guy from *The Daily Show* mixed up in such perverted silliness. I think he stammered out something and tried tying the whole experience into the insanity of voting against the Clean Water Act. They got what they needed and hopped off the bus as we approached Sixth Avenue, to begin heading north back to the studio.

We really were enjoying ourselves other than the now near-obsession I had for a cigarette. Psycho Mark briefly got off the bus and rode on the front grill yelling, "Gak Gak Gak" or something else irrelevant. I don't know why he did it, but at that point, if it didn't involve me getting nicotine into my system, I didn't give a shit. I also had an 8:00 p.m. gig in South Jersey. We were heading up Sixth, doing a couple of final call-ins to wrap up the day when we noticed anywhere between four and a thousand police cars with their lights flashing. Cops in white shirts were in the middle of the street, pointing at the bus to pull over. Naïve jackass that I was, I figured now I'd be able to hop off the bus and have a smoke.

Once the bus was stopped, a couple of officers briefly boarded and took fast stock of the situation. The only person they didn't notice was Psycho Mark, who told me he'd been in the bathroom allegedly flushing a twenty-year jail sentence down the toilet. As they waited for orders, Rick called in and I heard him stammer out to Opie the now infamous, "This is . . . this is legal, isn't it?" That was a very encouraging thing to hear from the producer. We've been overrun by police and he suddenly remembers he has a third grader's knowledge of the law. At this point in my relationship with

Opie & Anthony, I hadn't realized that when thinking of radio bits, the word "consequences" consistently slipped everyone's mind in the prep meetings.

The officers put plastic cuffs on all of us and escorted us off the bus past throngs of cheering fans and television cameras and onto a paddywagon. We began our trip to a precinct at the southern tip of the city, and while en route, Psycho Mark somehow slipped out of his cuffs and called the radio show. This jackass was giggling and carrying on like we were on our way to Jones beach instead of jail. Somehow the officers driving found out one of us had called the show and they were fucking pissed. The cops have always been fans of the show and arresting us certainly wasn't their decision. We found out later it came from Mayor Giuliani. Apparently, President Clinton was in town, and the Voyeur Bus was getting dangerously near the travel route designated by Secret Service, which embarrassed and pissed off the mayor. A bus full of teenage tits driving by Clinton's motorcade route; insert joke here (since I am obviously too lazy to bother).

Once in the station house we were processed and fingerprinted, while the captains and lieutenants tried to decide what to charge us with. The whole time we were in the station, I was looking across the room and trying to peek up Melanie's skirt. She was yapping and chitchatting and bugging everyone and I just loved her. By this point it had been about eight or nine hours since I smoked and I was ready to fucking scream. I finally understood the feeling of being willing to suck a cock for a drug. Mercifully, a lieutenant who spoke with Lewis and me did allow us to smoke in the station house. We had about five between us and sucked them down quickly.

He told us we'd probably be put through the system, which meant spending the night in the Tombs, the notoriously awful holding area in downtown Manhattan. I asked if Lewis and me would be able to stay together in a cell and he asked disgustedly, "Why, so you two can protect each other?" I realized, of course, that he was correct. In jail my idea of protecting Lewis would be to hold his glasses while he was juggling cocks with his mouth.

We wound up leaving the station house and indeed heading to the Tombs. The smell in there was sickening; sweat and vomit and shit, with the potential for a fractured jaw thrown in for good measure. The guards gave us our own cell. Nine guys, locked up for staring at tits on a bus. We were officially charged with "promoting the lewdness of a body," which is a misdemeanor so low it makes littering look like infanticide. As the hours dragged on and more prisoners began entering, we got moved into cells with them. None of them really bothered us; they knew what we were there for and were more interested in hearing about the girls and the tits and trashing Giuliani. Luckily, there were nine of us. Guys like Lewis and myself presented no real threat, but Steve C. is a strapping 320-pound Lebanese man with a horrible temper and a liver like Mickey Roarke's. (He *was* a 320-pound Lebanese man; since his stomach stapling he has become quite the featherweight.) The worst part of the Tombs, besides the awful food and smell and convicts and roaches, is the remarkably unpleasant condition of the toilets. At this point I would have given my kingdom for a clean toilet seat and fifteen hundred yards of Charmin. I had what felt like a world-record shit building up and letting it go in my pants was beginning to look like the best option.

As our time with the judge drew near, we were moved upstairs. It was now about 7:00 p.m. on Friday and we were in complete panic mode. If we weren't seen on Friday night, we'd have to stay there until Monday morning. We were finally put in smaller cells right outside the courtroom, four people to a cell. One of the prisoners in my cell told me that an old trick is to jam toilet paper up your ass when you have to take a dump. I appreciated the advice but was really trying to avoid things like sandbags and spackle; I just wanted to shit like a human being.

Once inside the court, our case was read and the judge not only threw out the charges, but scolded the prosecution for wasting everyone's time. And just that fast, it was over. I walked out of the courtroom and our lawyer told me that there was a Jim Norton wanted in another state for a sex crime (I neglected to ask if he was also a dick-joke comic with a weak chin) and that I should stop into a station house and clear up any potential for misunderstanding. I thanked him, walked out, and bought cigarettes. Nelson Mandela wasn't more relieved when he was freed. I lit up immediately and hopped into a cab because I had twenty minutes before I was scheduled to be onstage at Dangerfield's.

I made it to my shows and was then invited to a celebration thrown by a few female *O&A* listeners. I wanted to go badly, but I hadn't showered since Thursday morning and my balls smelled like Staten Island. And let's not forget that dump I was still struggling with. It had gotten to the point where I was afraid that if I sat on the bowl, the little Kintner boy was going to spill out all over the bathroom floor. So I politely declined so I could go home and shit in peace. Little did I realize that this *awful* experience had just made me an official member of the show and changed my career forever.

AN ENCHANTING EVENING

I HAD A long night tonight down at the Cellar; four sets that started at 8:10 p.m. and finished at two in the morning. I have a stupid cough, so I'm trying to get through my sets and I sound like a tuberculosis patient. Ray Romano and Kevin James went on the middle two shows together just to fuck around, and the crowd was thrilled to say the least. Nothing brings you back to reality like standing between two comics who have made more money this month than I'll make in my entire career.

I haven't been running around as much lately; I've been pretty lazy. It's always interesting standing outside the Cellar at 3:00 a.m.; you meet truly wonderful people. And there's also nothing quite as lovely as having your finger jammed up your nose and hearing someone say, "Yeah, him . . . he was on the Colin Quinn show." Not only do I have to end my booger hunt prematurely, but now I have to make small talk with this idiot and his girlfriend while we all pretend I didn't just have my finger scraping the inside of my skull. The whole time we're talking I can feel the juicy delight I was about to remove tickling my nostril hairs. I had partially dislodged it, so every time I uttered a word it would vibrate maddeningly. Mercifully, our chat was brief. It ended a few minutes later when this idiot wiped falafel off the corner of his mouth and then went to shake my hand. My finger was in my nose, he just wiped his mouth, and now he wanted to lock hands like blood brothers. I politely declined, saying I'd coughed into my hand and didn't want to get him sick. (Which was a big fat fib, of course. If I don't mind blasting syphilis into a girl's face, giving this asshole a cough would not concern me. It would, in fact, delight me.)

On my way home a short time later, my finger was still lazily meandering around my septum, and I pulled up to a red light behind a cab. A black transsexual got out of the cab, and as his friend was still paying the tab when the light turned green, of course, the cars behind me start *BLARING* on their horns, and this fucking douchebag started screaming at me. The other androgynous passenger got out, and as I drove away, daddy's disappointment #1 looked at me and screamed, "Stop beeping, you fucking faggot!" The irony of this was almost unbearable and the worst part about it was all I could manage to scream back out my window was, "I didn't do it!" What a marvelous, cutting comeback. Too bad I didn't have more time, I could have screamed, "I'm rubber, you're glue," or told him to, "Take a long walk off a short pier." *ANYTHING* would have been better than my panicked, meek, completely uncomic response. The one time in a year I needed my God-given wit and I respond like a five-year-old standing next to a broken lamp.

One thing that bugs me about doing stand-up is that I tend to feel like black people don't enjoy me, or when they do, it's fleeting and tentative. I am onstage on the late show, *KILLING*, and I looked over at the table of two black couples, and they were just staring. Not nasty or aggressively, just completely unentertained. They certainly understood the material. Is it because they don't relate to my personality? Or maybe it's that I'm an aggressive, opinionated, creepy white man with what is typically a Southern racist haircut? This is something I've noticed throughout my career. Maybe I just notice it more when they're black, because by far the worst hecklers or incidents have happened with white audience members. I've tried to figure out what it is. My material? My attitude? Or maybe it's my "Where's Jim Crow When You Need Him?" T-shirt. It's not something I'm obsessed with but it is a pattern I've noticed. I'm certainly not a bigot; as a matter of fact I go out of my way to shake black people's hands and tell them, "Hey, you're every bit as good as I am." Sometimes, I'll even stand next to an African-American, point to a Puerto Rican, and remark, "I'd much rather have you in my neighborhood than him." I try to be a man of the people and there are some folks who just don't appreciate that.

Incidentally, as I've been sitting here typing, I've cut about thirty farts. Some have been so bad I can't even enjoy them. They're the hot, quiet kind that come immediately after an unpleasant stomach rumble. Usually those are my favorites, but tonight they smell like spoiled vegetables. I can only wonder what's rotting in my colon. Well, I've covered boogers, racism, and farts. Quite remarkable, thought-provoking writing. I suck.

Keith Robinson, one of my *MANY* friends of color.

1986 NOTE I GOT FROM AN EX-GIRLFRIEND

THIS IS A letter I got from a girl I was dating at the end of 1985. I was a high school senior and she was a freshman or sophomore, I think. We were both virgins (we never did sleep together). Her family *hated* me and made her end the relationship because on New Year's Eve, I got completely drunk, did some pushups to get my veins bulging, and cut my wrist. I had done it many times before, but this particular time went badly and I had to get eighteen stitches. (These were all attention-seeking devices, by the way. I was a typical pukey, suburban, "woe is me" nerd.) Obviously, the most amazing and unbelievable thing about the incident is that I did some pushups.

I don't remember if she and I ever got back together; I continued drinking and partying for almost another year, until February 1987. This letter just made me laugh because it reminded me of what a social pariah I really was.

3/17/86

Jimby,

The entire time I went out with this girl she called me Jimby. Almost any other nickname would have been more acceptable—Meat Tits, Diarrhea Mouth and Faggot included.

Hey Babes! How ya been? *Well, I attempted suicide recently, but aside from that, things are peachy.* I haven't heard from you in a while. *Maybe it's because I was in rehab after another wrist-slicing episode, you silly goose. Either that or I was taking a forty-day shit and couldn't get to the phone.* I called you Saturday night, but, you weren't home. *Good use of commas.* I like you soo much I wish we didn't break up. I have an important Question for you. *You know it's an important question when the Q is capitalized. Capital letters always call for emphasis and I'm glad this Idiot understood that.* Well, actually it's a plan. I would like to know if we could go back out w/each other but under other conditions. like it would have to be that we could only see each other in school, or if <u>noone</u> was home over my house or j——s maybe; and that I would have to call you. *This sounds fantastic! There's nothing a boyfriend fresh out of rehab craves more than to be hidden away like stolen loot or a canker sore.* It may not sound too good but it's better than what we have now. *To be honest, it sounds downright awful. If you'd like something "better than what we have now" how about tongue bathing my ballbag and fingering my tush?* I wish I could explain how much I want to go back out w/you but it would take tooo long. Well Jimmy I gotta go and I'll write again. I'm gonna try and call you tonite about 11-10:30 p.m. *Nothing displays complete idiocy more than listing the later time first.* Gotta go. W/B/S

Luv, A——

P.S. Think about what I asked you about before you give me an answer. Who did you have for biology? *Now that the niceties are out of the way, let's get to the meat of the issue, shall we? Who's teaching you about frog testicles this year? And before you open more veins in a tub, don't forget to mention what period you have lunch.*

3/17/86

Jimby,

Hey Babes! How ya been? I haven't heard from you in a while. I called you Saturday night, but, you weren't home. I like you soo much I wish we didn't break up. I have an important question for you. Well, actually it's a plan. I would like to know if we could go back out w/ eachother but under other conditions. like it would be that we could only see eachother in school, or if no one was home over my house or ~~-~~ maybe; and that I would have to call you. It may not sound too good but it's better than what we have now. I wish I could explain how much I want to go ~~to~~ back out w/ you but it would take too long. Well Jimmy I gotta go and I'll write again. I'm gonna try and call you tonite about 11-10:30 pm. Gotta go. W/B/S

P.S. Think about what I asked you before you give me an answer.

Luv

Who do/did you have for biology?

The worst attempt at reconciliation ever attempted by anyone.

"GLENGARRY GLEN ROSS" AND *THE* SEARCH FOR HAWKEYE

I'VE NEVER BEEN a big fan of Broadway plays. "Not a big fan" is perhaps misleading, because it implies that I've been to one. I think the last play I went to was *Of Mice and Men*, which was put on in a small New Jersey theater when I was around thirteen. I fell in love with the movie starring Burgess Meredith and Lon Chaney Jr., so my grandmother got us tickets. Most boys that age are discovering girls. Most boys. Me? I preferred palling around with seventy-year-old women and watching low-budget productions of depressing books featuring retards getting their non-existent brains shot out in the final scene. A guy named Tom Noonan (who I saw years later in *Easy Money* with Rodney Dangerfield and Joe Pesci) played Lenny. It wasn't what I was hoping for. I'd seen the movie and wanted Lon Chaney Jr.'s interpretation of the character, *God-fucking-dammit*. I had no idea that someone else playing Lenny would do it differently. I sulked out of the theater and unsuccessfully tried to get my grandmother to jerk me off in the car.

Television has always been my main form of entertainment, second only to phoning in bomb threats to the White House in pig Latin. *M.A.S.H.* was by far my favorite show. I *loved* Hawkeye Pierce. Alan Alda evolved Hawkeye into the deepest and most complex character in the history of sitcoms. He was one of those rare characters on television who could make you laugh and cry with the same integrity. (Quick! Someone shove a cock in this kid's mouth and save him the humiliation of writing "laugh and cry" again.) I think you get the point. I love Alan Alda, one of my longest-standing heroes. I was on a daisy chain in a Chelsea men's room one afternoon when

I heard he was starring in *Glengarry Glen Ross* on Broadway. I immediately got tickets, then tried calling in any connections I had to arrange a face-to-face hello with him. Nothing panned out, so I unhappily accepted the fact that this was going to be a major undertaking.

I began scouting the place out like I was about to knock off an armored car. I stopped by the theater every day for about a week, but never saw Alan or any of the other actors coming or going. He is a notoriously difficult guy to get a picture with ("skittish" is the word I've often heard), but I figured if I stood outside after shows let out, there'd be an opportunity for a photo. I was sorely mistaken.

Day one of my pathetic scouting expedition, I saw a commotion outside of the theater next door. I ran over to see, hoping it was something funny like a heart attack or police tasering. No such luck; turns out it was Billy Crudup signing autographs. I had no idea who he was, but recognized that he was famous (whenever I see a guy being mobbed and signing things, my celebrity antennae intuitively goes up). So I walked over with my camera and in true weasely fashion, claimed to be a big fan. It would have been pretty easy to bust me; if he had said, "Really? Name one thing I've done," I'd have been royally fucked in the ass with the embarrassment stick. I've since learned he was in *Almost Famous*, which I did see and like. I still have no fucking idea who he is, though.

I glanced over and noticed Jeff Goldblum signing about five feet away. Well, now I was excited because I legitimately like Goldblum, although I prefer his earlier work. *Independence Day* was cute, but to see him braining a woman with a blackjack yelling, "Goddamn rich cunt!" in the original *Death Wish* is obviously untoppable. I was all by my lonesome, so I asked some girl if she could snap a picture of us. She sighed and had a look on her face like I just asked if I could knock her up for a few stem cells. This panicking bitch takes my camera and snaps an awful shot of me in the vicinity of Jeff. I am staring dumbly into the camera while he looks down at something he's signing for another fan.

Heather Mills could have taken a nicer photo with her fucking stump so I decided to continue lurking uncomfortably until I finally got his attention for real. Jeff eventually looked over at the pale blob in his peripheral and the unthinkable happened; he recognized me. Turns out he was a *Tough Crowd* fan. That was the first time a celebrity I genuinely liked knew who I was at a quick glance. We chatted for a few minutes about the show and its

Two close friends sharing a moment.

cancellation. He couldn't remember Colin Quinn's name, which brought me a feeling I can only describe as delicious rapture. I felt the energy of this magical conversation winding down; at one point there was a seven-minute silence that was filled only by awkward throat clearing and us staring at each other, so I began to panic internally. I didn't want the moment to end. Then suddenly it came to me that Goldblum was a huge Jim Florentine fan. He loved Special Ed on *Crank Yankers* and that fucking "Yaaayyyy,

The above photo featuring a lot of ceiling and not a lot of chin was the end of my day in the theater district. I went back a couple more times but to no avail; Alan Alda was nowhere to be found.

yaaayyyyy, I got mail, yaaayyyyy" has a higher recognition factor than the theme music from *Jaws*. I was living with him when he created that character on his *Terrorizing Telemarketers* CD (originally named Retard, changed to Special Ed for Comedy Central), so I mentioned this to Jeff, expecting some sort of party favors to fall out of the ceiling. He asked me to say hi to Jim for him and then promptly lost interest in me again.

The show I actually had tickets for finally rolled around and, of course, I couldn't get a girl to go with me. What the fuck did I expect? It's a play about real estate salesmen and I'm wondering why my e-mail isn't being spammed by big-titted party girls vying for that extra seat. In true loser fashion, I was scrambling to find anyone who would come see this play. And it wasn't that I needed the companionship, I simply needed a two-handed person who could aim a fucking camera. After an endless string of shitty excuses from women ("I have to wash my hair," "Love to but I'm committing suicide in an hour," "I'm babysitting a forty-year-old man with Down's syndrome," etc.) I finally settled on Steve C. Despite being a rage-swallowing Lebanese bear, he's something of a well-rounded individual, one of those guys who are equally comfortable sitting through a play, or taking Cialis and watching Al-Zarqawi beheading videos. In the spirit of honesty I have to admit, he really was a fine date. We had quite a lovely homoerotic afternoon (you know, two men in a dark theater just eating Twizzlers, staring straight ahead while their legs touch and they pretend not to notice). The play was very good although I enjoyed the movie more. Uh-oh, looks like someone's developing a little pattern here. . . .

Once the play ended, Steve and I quickly pulled up our trousers and headed outside to cover the exits. Luckily for us there were only two: one by the main entrance and a long, back exit hallway. I figured the back hallway would be my best shot at seeing Alan, although an older gentleman on the scene informed me that he always left through the other door and hopped right into a car. Fuck you, fella, I thought to myself. The first one out the door was Gordon Clapp (*NYPD Blue*), who played the roll of Dave. He was very cordial and took a photo with me, and he came out the back hallway door, as I had predicted the actors would. That older gentleman could take a flying leap into a shit pile as far as I was concerned. Jeffrey Tambor also came out from the aforementioned hallway, walking his bike. He really didn't want to stop but the Oliver Twist look on my fat face guilted him into smiling for a picture before he rode off.

Tom Wopat really threw a monkey wrench into things when he left through the smaller door near the main exit. FUCK FUCK FUCK! Now what? I can't cover two doors and Steve is borderline retarded. I approached Tom for a photo, although secretly I thought *The Dukes of Hazard* was hillbilly drivel. However, while posing together, I glanced through the stage door and noticed none other than Alan Alda lurking in the background near the door. A cuntbag security guard moved me and everyone else back as a black town car pulled up. After the guard moved us back, I began inching closer to the stage door again. At this point I felt like John Hinckley, Jr., and if I had a gun, I'd have shot that faggoty guard on principle. Without warning Alda lasers from the door into the car. I heard he was skittish but for fuck's sake he bolted like a ferret with a bottle rocket crammed up his dumper. Right into the car, not even an acknowledgment that people were waiting. Even if he wasn't stopping, he could have at least waved or thrown up a gang sign. I never saw that power-hungry security guard again, but I hope he developed testicular cancer in both eyes. The next time I had any shot at all at a meeting would be a few months later at a book signing in Los Angeles.

I got a call from Yoshi, my potty-mouthed Asian comedian friend who also prints porn DVDs for a living. He informed me about an Alda book signing so I went online and bought a copy. We showed up and were about eightieth in line out of 150 people. Nice turnout, but not exactly Woodstock. Once in line we were handed our books as well as a flier that said Mr. Alda could be photographed but would *not* pose for pictures or look up for one. *Or look up for one?* Fucking Christ, I am all for not putting a guy out, but looking up and saying "Cheese!" isn't exactly backbreaking work. So we stood in line for ninety minutes or so and I was getting increasingly irritated as we worked our way into the store. *Won't even look up for a photograph* was bouncing around inside of my head and making me want to scream (or more accurately, cry and beg).

Finally, it was my time to get my book signed. Almost thirty years of hero worship and here I was, handing my book to Alan Alda, in the flesh. The

This was the first pic snapped by Yoshi, who was *panicking* by this time.

great Hawkeye Pierce was a foot away from me. Yoshi and I had planned on him snapping the shot of me as Alan signed my book and I leaned in to talk to him. Getting him to look up and into the camera was the goal. I was a nervous nelly and stammered out some dreck about how much I loved him and that I was a comedian and that I was in a sitcom coming out on HBO and blah blah blah blah. Just a weak-chinned, blathering idiot. He was surprisingly nice and acted flattered that another performer was doting over him. He smiled, we shook hands, and it was a pleasant chat; I knew I'd get him to look up for a photo.

At first glance, this appears to be a photo of me lecturing Alan on the benefits of invading people's personal space. The guy running the event, a bespectacled, mousey little douchebag, kept trying to hustle me along. This guy was just another mall security–type dickhead who was trying to wield a little power. I had absolutely no respect for this piece of shit, but his incessant pestering was making Yoshi nervous. Of course, being rattled like that caused him to continually misfire on the camera. Right after this shitty, ill-timed shot, Alan and I shook hands and I got him to look at the camera. So much for that fucko flier and its stern warnings; he looked up and smiled! The problem was that nervous-ass Yoshi couldn't get the camera to snap at the right moment. I wanted to fucking *scream*. And I didn't want to scream at Yoshi (who handles pressure worse than Herman Munster) but rather at that four-eyed asshole who picked *now* to make up for a lifetime of boot licking and put on his Bossy Manager costume.

The Bookstore Gestapo'd had enough and finally told us to just leave. I quickly had to decide between slinking out the back door and killing a nerd in front of my childhood hero. I opted to just mutter, "Die," a bunch of times and walk out.

Now Yoshi and I were in a pitch-black parking lot behind the place. After every person got their book signed, they came down the same steps

As soon as Alan looked back down and we stopped shaking hands, Yoshi snapped this gem. At this point, I look like I'm telling him to march outside so I can kick his old ass.

we did and walked past us into the abyss. My goal was to lurk back here until Alan and his agent walked out, and then either get my picture, or set Yoshi on fire in protest. We were hedging our bets that he'd even leave this way as opposed to the front door. Sooner or later, I knew the manager would come out and kick us off the property. After an endless amount of time and unbearable, polite banter with strangers, *finally*, Alan came down the stairs. Initially, he tried to walk right past us and blow me off for the photo. He only stopped when I blurted out that I was the comedian from inside and even then he almost kept going. I knew we only had one shot at this and luckily, Yoshi was lined up and ready to go. It was a better shot than I ever could have hoped for, especially since I stepped on Alan's foot while we were getting into position. Smooth, Asian Yoshi made up for his earlier Parkinson's fuckup and took the perfect picture. It was well worth the wait and hassle; I love the fact that we're both front and center and smiling.

Well, one of us was smiling. Closer examination reveals that he was in fact *gritting his fucking teeth*. Nice to know that not only did I cause a scene at his signing and step on his foot, I ruined his entire evening. Sorry, Alan. And by the way, *Never Have Your Dog Stuffed: And Other Things I've Learned* is funny, poignant, and honest. I really loved it.

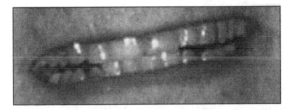

THE JACUZZI BLUES

I SPENT THE weekend in Las Vegas with my girlfriend, which was an odd choice because she doesn't enjoy gambling or prostitution. I had a gig in Caesar's Palace and figured it would be nice to finally bring a significant other to a hotel that doesn't look like a meth dealer was just stabbed in the lobby. Because the gig was for HBO, I was given a fancy suite (or more accurately, a suite that would have been fancy in 1966 when the hotel was built). It had two adjoining rooms with the bed and a bathroom in one, a living room and second bathroom in the other. The first thing we noticed was that the room stunk like smoke, so I tried the old trick of taking a giant shit on the rug and then calling housekeeping up and asking, "What in Sam Hill is this??" Normally a fresh dump on the floor will get you moved to another room with a complimentary fruit basket. However, in this case, the hotel was sold out, so the maid just scooped up the soft, buttery pile with her bare hands, dropped it onto the coffee table, and sculpted a unicorn out of it. We also noted that the furniture in the living room had what appeared to be a bevy of cum stains covering it. (Unfortunately those were not of my doing. I made a mental note to shoot a load on the sofa cushions the next time I needed a room change. Nice touch.)

One unexpected feature of the room was the Jacuzzi in the middle of the bedroom. This is obviously tacky and very Vegasy, but nonetheless we found it to be a lovely surprise. Much to our glee, we soon discovered a second, larger Jacuzzi in the living-room bathroom. This was shaping up to be a quite the classy room, jizz stains and all. My best gal and I celebrated by stretching our arms straight out, holding hands, and spinning in a circle as we alternately laughed and threw up.

Incidentally, this trip to Vegas marks the first time I have ever flown somewhere with a girlfriend. And the trip almost started out on the wrong foot because at the last minute stupid Continental Airlines switched my seat so we weren't sitting together. When I asked the woman-robot behind the counter why, she gave the standard answer of "the aircraft was changed." I knew she was lying because it's what employees in this despicable industry do: They lie. And it's nothing specific they lie about, it's everything. The idea of actually dealing with a nonscreaming customer as an equal never occurs to any of these shitfaces. So I figured I would check at the gate. When I got to the gate, there was a middle-aged fat frog with glasses moping behind the counter. I actually had to turn this thing over and open its legs to verify gender. It was a female and when I asked it about the seat switch it gave me the *same fucking lie* I was told earlier. And I know it was a lie because on my itinerary we were scheduled to fly on a 757-300 and we were still on a 757-300. When I pointed this out, Miss Genderless Frog Cunt got all huffy and said that didn't matter. Didn't matter? So they switched from one 757-300 to another, the exact same fucking aircraft, and found it necessary to move my seat? (I really have come to loathe the detached smugness of airline employees.) I hated this woman's guts and to show my displeasure, I sincerely thanked her as I maintained eye contact while eating a booger.

Once on the plane, we asked a well-spoken black fellow to switch seats. I made up some lie about how we were on our way to raise money for the NAACP and needed to be next to each other to strategize. I told him "we was good white folk" and he should do us a solid. He understood where I was coming from and we gave each other a knowing wink as he headed to what was supposed to be my seat. She and I sat down and began making out immediately. Before we even backed out of the gate, I was scolded twice by the flight attendant for fingering my girlfriend under the blanket. She is just one of those people I always have fun with, whether we're laughing over an Amber alert or blowing baloney burps into each other's faces.

The only real monkey wrench in the weekend was her period. I realize women get them, I'm not implying it makes them dirty. It certainly does make them into quite the cranky pants, though. She almost bit my head off when I suggested she sleep on the floor so she didn't kill the fun vibe by hemorrhaging all over the comforter in the middle of the night. To make up for my faux pas, I surprised her with a singing telegram and we were right as rain again. There is just something about a slender, shirtless man with a bow tie standing in a hotel doorway singing "Philadelphia" that makes a dame putty in your hands.

One major difference in our personalities is her openness and comfort with her own body. A decade of Pilates and manic depression have translated into a trim waist and superior abs. Down at the hotel pool, all eyes were on her as she strutted around in her see-through white macro bikini. Flirting is an art form for her; whenever she catches a fellow grabbing a gander she winks, twirls in a circle, and does the Cabbage Patch for at least a minute. Public pools have always been an esteem-destroyer for me, so I opted to dress discreetly in a velour sweat suit and full-length leather trench. Incidentally, don't misinterpret flirty as disrespectful; no matter how many guys at a party tickle her labia or do lines off her tits, I always know she's leaving with me.

The worst part of dating a girl who's in shape is that at times you have to be naked in front of her. I try to avoid it whenever possible by wearing a T-shirt or carefully positioning myself behind furniture whenever I'm nude. Occasionally she'll light a candle so we can take a sexy, romantic shower together. By the third shower she started requesting I take off my shirt once we begin soaping each other up. As I alluded to in my first book, *The Burden of Man Tits*, I am fairly self-conscious about my body, so normally when the shower subject comes up I fake a spinal cord injury or claim one of my parents just died. Well, now I had a dilemma because there was not one but two Jacuzzis. How could I possibly justify not enjoying a romantic bubble bath with my beautiful girlfriend? I was so uncomfortable I even tried coming out of the closet to her but she wouldn't hear of it. I finally gave in to the idea once we came to the silent agreement that I'd be rewarded with a deep ass licking. Yet again the subject of her menstruation came up, and she ultimately decided not to remove her tampon, saving us the humiliation of resembling two potatoes floating in beet stew. I was assigned the task of running the water and of course I ran it way too hot. My girl walks in wearing nothing but the sexy platform shoes she picked out for her birthday. (I mean it when I say these things are fucking sexy. They're seven inches high and transparent with live catfish swimming in the heels.) Standing knee-deep in the water she playfully chides me for the temperature by alternately splashing me and slapping my face with a rubber cock she's brought along for the occasion.

By far, the worst part of getting into a scalding Jacuzzi is using my hands to cover my cock and balls. First, I lower myself to the thighs, breathing rapidly and screaming *"Oh, help me Lawdy!"* at full volume until security knocks on the door. Step two, and this is the toughie, is slooooowwwwly submerging my crotch while removing my protective fingers. In this position my hands are occupied so I have no way to hide my blubbery stomach while squatting. My girl's in the tub looking in shape and fuckable as I squat and groan like an African woman giving birth. We kissed as I uncomfortably hovered with my minuscule genitals begging me to stand and give them some cool air. While running the bath I took a page out of her playbook and lit two scented candles (cinnamon yard-ape and vanilla cadaver). In all honesty, I was hoping the effects of the flickering flame would give me the illusion of physical fitness. However, the shadow on the wall painted a different picture: Alfred Hitchcock stealing a kiss while shitting in a trough.

Fast forward five minutes and two failed lovemaking attempts later, we're both climbing uneventfully out of the Jacuzzi. I'm rubbing aloe on my tender red scrotum and she's in a shitty mood because the fish in both of her shoes died.

DIRK

ONCE AGAIN I am sitting in an airport, which lately seems to be the opening to every chapter. I am flying to Atlanta and we were supposed to leave at 6:25 p.m., but due to thunderstorms we're delayed until 9:40 p.m. (I wish some of my friends were here so I could get some big laughs saying things like, "Seems like a real case of 'hurry up and wait.'" Whenever I say things like that it really cracks everybody up. Like before, I was on line purchasing some bubble gum when a fellow asked me, "So how you doin'?" to which I fired back, "I'd complain, but who the heck would listen?" We shared a good laugh over that one, and then he followed me into the men's room, pushed me into the handicap stall, and forced me to eat his ass at knifepoint. I never actually saw the knife but he hinted he had one, and in this crazy world I wasn't taking any chances.

After it was all over I wiped my tears away and then he made me help him back into his wheelchair and push him to his gate. He told me that if I went to the authorities he'd call my parents and tell them I was asking for it by wearing tight-fitting slacks while chomping my gum loudly and winking. I knew not to cross Dirk (his name is actually Seth, but I like calling him Dirk) because he was a man who meant business. So I got him his paper and coffee from Starbucks and waited for his flight to board. Dirk lost both of his legs during a botched robbery of a Meals on Wheels truck in the early 1980s. To make his living now, he fills both his prosthetics with rare marmalades and sells them on the black market overseas. As Dirk's flight began to board he gave me one more dire warning, "Remember . . . snitches get stitches," and then we made out for a few minutes until he left.

I get weak in the knees when he rhymes like that and he knows it. Not to mention his breath, which smelled lightly of Starbucks coffee, plaque, and the urinal cake he'd been gnawing on.

I am happy to report that I finally made a good decision. When checking in I almost switched to the earlier flight, which was also delayed but would have gotten me in to Atlanta ninety minutes earlier than my scheduled flight. I decided not to switch because I didn't think my luggage would make it. Remember the gorilla who used to jump up and down on the Samsonite suitcase? He now works in Newark Airport as a baggage handler. I figured I could kill the extra wait time by hanging out in the men's room and working on my new children's pop-up book about testicular cancer.

So the earlier flight boarded and then about forty minutes later they made all the passengers get off the plane. Apparently, the crew became "illegal" because they'd been on the ground too long. I don't understand the "illegal" classification. Maybe at a certain hour the whole crew turns Mexican. They all grow foreskins and thick, kissable lips, their hair turns jet-black, and they suddenly have seventy extra people living in their one-bedroom apartment. Of course, I am just being a silly little angel; you can't instantly become Mexican, it takes time (a very little-known fact is that Mexicans aren't born, they're created when you cut Dominicans in half).

Whatever it means, the passengers were absolutely fuming because they had to stand on line getting off the plane to be checked in to the flight I was on. And to broach another familiar subject, I was in the bathroom virtually nonstop. I took three nice dumps, which I attributed to the greasy artichoke and spinach dip I had for lunch in the Friday's in Terminal A. Before I resigned myself to using the airport men's room for something other than a social club, I sat alone in a row of seats and cut somewhere in the neighborhood of three hundred putrid, horrendous gassers. I have *never* wanted a travel companion as badly as I did today;

to not share those pungent gifts with someone was truly a waste.

I remember in the fall of last year Florentine and I were traveling to Vegas together for a gig. We had both been upgraded to first class due to our frequent-flyer status. Naturally, we sat together and I was in rare form. I farted so much on that flight I actually became embarrassed. They were the type of farts you need in first class too; quiet, hot, and reeking of rotting meat. We were in seats 1A and 1B, the first two seats on the plane. Jim got up to use the bathroom and I dropped a particularly abominable one. The flight attendants in the galley said something to the other flight attendant and she got some scented spray and started to blast the outside of the bathroom door. She thought that dumb Florentine's shit fumes were leaking out of the bathroom and into the cabin. She must have been six feet away from me and she still got a nice noseful. It should go without saying, but I was giggling uncontrollably. For the rest of the flight I fired them out and one flight attendant literally stopped in his tracks, backtracked, and got the spray. He sprayed in the aisle next to me. They all knew it was us, as everyone else was revolted and we were holding newspapers up in front of our faces and laughing so hard we were shaking. I had one more and I knew it was bad because I could feel its warmth while it was still working its way through my plumbing. The plane had landed and we all stood up to get off, and Jim was whispering for me to let it rip, but I finally chickened out. No one was moving, we were all standing in the aisle, and I knew it would smell dreadful. I wasn't afraid that it would stink, but I knew I wouldn't be able to not laugh. The flight attendants were so fucking completely disgusted with us I honestly thought one more would get me reported as having behaved rudely on the plane and maybe hurt my upgrade status. Who knows? I should have done it, but I was a coward. What a badge of honor: to fart so much and so horribly that you lose your frequent-flyer status.

Jim was on a plane with Stuttering John and some other comics and caused such a ruckus by farting loudly that one of the flight attendants scolded him and threatened to tell the captain if he didn't stop. I can't tell the story because it's Jim's and I wasn't there, but it's one of the greatest fart stories ever.

So back to my original point: I made the right decision by not switching flights. For a while my stomach was threatening queasiness, which I think is the same type of psychosomatic shit that happens when I perform sometimes. It seems like whenever I am presented with any sort of frightening or uncomfortable situation I do what any real man does: get the urge to vomit or have noxious fumes seep out of my keister.

We are finally on the plane and in the air. My stomach still feels a bit cruddy and I'd like to just nap a bit but I can't because the broad sitting next to me has her fucking overhead reading light on. I normally don't mind that, but the bulb for this thing was obviously taken off the front of a tractor trailer. It is incredibly irritating and keeping me awake. I feel like taking out my dick, covering it with my blanket, then uncovering it slightly until she looks over. As soon as she sees it I'll cover it again and continue playing this game of peek-a-boo until she kisses the helmet or turns off her goddamn light. I tried to eat on the flight but wouldn't you know it; the meal was a Reuben sandwich. My still-queasy stomach needs a Reuben like a burn victim needs a vinegar daiquiri. I have to piss again; I've already annoyed the bookworm twice by getting up and I fully intend to barrel by her again in about ten seconds.

We landed at close to 1:00 a.m. Then I had to get my bags and walk out to the lot to meet my ride. On the way to find my driver, a tall black man asked me if I needed a ride. I told him I had a car service picking me up and he insisted he could drive me. He wasn't offering in some homoerotic way, he was a livery driver wanting to make cash. He walked me down to the lot, where I saw another larger black man standing by a car. The guy walking with me looked like Delroy Lindo and all I could think was that I was going to be beaten and robbed in this shitty parking lot in Atlanta by West Indian Archie and an accomplice. Luckily my driver was right there as well, so I got into the car without incident. This creep hung outside the door hoping for a tip, and to my credit, I gave him nothing. It's times like this I wish Dirk were around to protect me.

A DISASTER MOVIE! PART 1

I FINALLY SAW *The Day After Tomorrow* this week. I realize it's a few years old, and I only bought it because I needed two legit movies to sandwich the she-male trilogy I was taking up to the counter. As far as disaster movies go, it wasn't bad. The special effects were amazing with the typical cheesedick story line. I am writing a similar film (about a second ice age due to global warming), but in my version, instead of it taking weeks, it takes almost twelve thousand years. The change in oceanic currents is noticed by Ted Frutz, an oceanographer living in Southern California twice convicted of dry humping the face of an invalid. Ted immediately calls the office of Mayor Lance Blark and tells him that if they don't act immediately, life as we know it could change for good by the year 14004. There is an aerosol can–spraying party scheduled for that week and Ted is adamant that it be stopped. He is concerned about the frailty of the ozone layer. Mayor Blark tells Ted that his theory is hogwash and that Ted should go suck a fat baby's dick, which confuses Ted. (Does the mayor want him to suck a baby dick that is fat or the dick of a fat baby? Playing it safe, he does both.)

He then goes on to explain to Ted that the annual spray-can bonanza brings in an estimated $400 for the township in hotel expenses alone. "How are we supposed to replace that money, Ted? Are you going to come up with it?" challenges the mayor. Ted counters that he is most certainly not going to come up with it, he only has $70 in the bank, and that is set aside to treat his testicular psoriasis. Mayor Blark tries to make a joke about Ted's perpetually scaly scrotum, but Ted interrupts and tells the mayor he's a fiscally irresponsible cunt who should die in a hotel fire.

Enter Maggie Scolchirk, a sultry, sexy Swedish scientist who recently had a mastectomy. This wouldn't be noticeable if she didn't insist on wearing transparent bikini tops. She read about Ted's global warming/ocean current–change theory in an online chat room dedicated to amputees who are concerned with atmospheric conditions. A fellow chat-room junkie, Mark Therbins, tells her in great detail about Ted and the bureaucratic resistance he faced. It takes three weeks to convey the story in its entirety, as Mark has no arms or hands and has to type with his shoulder stumps. He is constantly making spelling errors due to the fact he pushes eleven keys at a time. Maggie hates talking to Mark, especially when he attempts cybersex. One time in the middle of a heated debate over the relationship between cumulus clouds and the armed robbery rate in black neighborhoods, Mark begins to get fresh. Maggie tries to be understanding and gently keep the conversation on the appropriate track. She's not attracted to Mark and besides, he continually spells "cunt" with a *Q*.

It was early Tuesday morning when Ted's secretary, Mrs. Edna Beezeneedle, walked in with the message. Mrs. Beezeneedle is a fiftysomething, slightly overweight, yet gregarious gal. She thinks Ted is out of this world and laughs good-naturedly at everything he says. (This is normally quite the compliment, although it irritated Ted two years ago when he told Mrs. Beezeneedle that both of his children were killed in a water slide accident and she guffawed uncontrollably.) Today, Ted hardly noticed her enter; he was busy painting a FUCK MAYOR BLARK WITH A STICK sign for the upcoming Kiwanis Club parade. He had spent the previous night distributing flyers that read AEROSAL CANS ARE FOR FAGGOTS! The flyers then went on to explain how the ozone layer currently has a hole in it larger than JFK's head and if we didn't smarten up as a society, in a few thousand years we'd be knee-deep in dog shit with nothing but a baby spoon. As was customary when he was working, she placed the note down by the John Wayne Gacy figurine on his desk and walked back out of the office without saying a word. Ted absently picked up the note at his leisure. *Ted, a scientist named Maggie Scolchirk called. She agrees with your theory and would like to meet at an afterhours bar in Compton to talk about it. She thinks that you're wrong about the time frame, though, and that we may only have eight or nine thousand years. She wants you to call ASAP. Edna. P.S. I whipped up a batch of that roast beef ice cream you love so much.*

"Eight or nine thousand years? Shit, that really puts us up against the wall." Ted was deep in thought in a corner booth at JB's, a popular neighborhood bar in Compton that specialized in Colt 45 and pickled pigs feet. He didn't notice her come in until he heard whistles and voices shouting, "White bitch," and "Where's the other titty?" She sat down and was immediately impressed with him. He was a man in his late thirties; distinguished looking, yet comfortable enough to wear a SHIT HAPPENS headband with a three-piece suit. Yup, this Ted sure was a tall drink of water. Ted had the same feelings about Maggie. He loved her beautiful face, her pouty, almost cleft pallet lip, and her long blond Swedish locks. And as a devout breast man, he really loved the way her tits . . . "*What the fuck?*" Ted screamed while shaking his fists up and down.

"What's the matter, Ted?" asked a now panic-stricken Maggie.

"Oh, did I say that out loud?" Ted stammered out uncomfortably. "Ha, ha, silly me. My grandmother called me this morning; she fell down the steps and shattered her hip. She asked me to call an ambulance and I forgot." This seemed to relax Maggie and they got down to the business at hand. Maggie explained how she felt the changing ocean currents would melt the ice caps (and staring at her chest, Ted could easily imagine those old ice caps; one standing tall and firm and one melted away into a bra full of mush) and that they needed to do something. Newly inspired and trying to impress her, Ted leaped to his feet and shouted, "I'm going to tell the president!"

Unfortunately, other patrons in the bar thought he said, "I've got dead presidents," so as he was walking out the door, they caved in his skull with a car battery and stole his wallet.

TO BE CONTINUED . . .

HAPPY BIRTHDAY, DEAR FLORENTINE

I SPENT MOST of last night in Jersey with Florentine, celebrating his fortieth birthday. (Just to crack everyone up, when I saw him I said good-naturedly, "You don't look a day over forty-five." Lines like that set the wild tone for the party.) I had been in Vegas performing and was invited to stay one more night for the Pimps and Hoes party, which I hated to miss. Since I put most of these pimps in Escalades, I felt it would be nice to mingle. My decision to fly back was based simply on the fact that Jim hired Sabbra Cadabra to play at his party. They are a Black Sabbath tribute band who I've heard on CD but never seen live.

The party was held in an Elk's Lodge (as most upper-echelon shindigs are) in an awful part of South Jersey. It was perfect. I realized I had forgotten to get Jim a gift, so I gave him the Rodney Dangerfield autobiography I had stolen in the Vegas airport. I was quite enjoying it so this was more of a sacrifice than it sounds like. I knew a lot of the people there; some were comics, some were Jim's family, and a shitload of his weirdo friends, most of whom I've met. The party started at seven and I arrived fashionably late at 7:03. The first person I saw was Club Soda Kenny, who was just standing there making people uncomfortable. He looked divine in his snug, form-fitting T-shirt, and I am not afraid to admit that when I saw his arms I thought of how comforting they'd be to have wrapped around me in a thunderstorm. I was happy to see him and we gave each other the secret handshake. I can't give it away; but think "two-fisted Dirty Sanchez."

Chuck Mignanelli came over to say hello. Chuck is a friend and a comic who originally hails from Pittsburgh, which is a fine city if you

187

like steel mills and incest. Like Kenny, he is a large, broad-shouldered fellow. However, Kenny is mustachioed, while Chuck is clean-shaven with penetrating blue eyes. Chuck is outwardly a relatively normal guy for a comic until you examine him a bit closer. He is somewhat claustrophobic and absolutely refuses to get on elevators; he would rather run up stairs instead. My one goal in life is to rent him a penthouse apartment just to watch him attempt sophistication while traipsing up and down fifty flights of steps. Chuck is a true horse's ass from western Pennsylvania.

The mood was very festive and everyone was eating meatballs and pasta. Members of the band were beginning to bring in their equipment as we all milled about aimlessly. I saw some people I haven't seen in quite a while, like Wayno Draino, a comedian/artist/writer who for years would eat vomit at parties. He has since mellowed and we chatted for a bit, he's quite a lovely gentleman when he isn't launching intestinal bile on someone.

I've gotten to know a lot of Jim's old friends from going to Ozzfest together every year. There's Boomer, a very in-shape suburban psychopath who looks like Peter North if he decided to sell stocks instead of shooting gallons of bleach-scented Silly String into the faces of runaways. Ishk is another one of Florentine's lifelong friends, and an hour into the party he was in the middle of the dance floor in a blackout with his pants and underwear around his ankles, holding two beers over his head. Tony was a bit more subdued than normal; I was hoping he'd find someone passed out to give the infamous "crack finger" to. When someone would pass out drunk, Tony would insert his finger into his own ass then hold it under the nose of the passed out person until they woke up from the stench (similar to a Dirty Sanchez without the actual under-the-nose rub). Unfortunately, I never witnessed any of these incidents, and am only passing on information that was given to me by Jim.

With Vos and Florentine in 1994. Sorry, Don, for decapitating you.

Our buddy Don Jamieson was in attendance. For those of you who've seen the *Meet the Creeps* DVD, Don is the other guy who stars with Jim. I love Don, although when I saw what was on his feet, I wanted to brain him with a candy dish. I happened to look down and notice he was wearing open-toed, slipperlike sandals. These were the type of sandals that just have a piece of leather going across the top of the foot so the toes poke through unobstructed. I was trying to enjoy the music and this idiot is dressed for a suicide bombing. Everyone else had on sneakers or shoes and he was sporting footwear that should come with a Koran and flight school coupons. I wouldn't have minded them as much if his toes weren't so irritatingly long; it was like standing next to a fucking Sleestack. The first four toes kind of dangled over the front of the sandal and then inexplicably, the little toe stopped growing when he was three weeks in the womb. Either that or he's a member of some European mafia that requires little toe severing to prevent police infiltration. I've never seen such a difference in toe length and the more I stared at them, the more I wanted to grind my heel into his bare tootsies while biting his face. Don has been a close friend for a decade, but from this day forth I will refuse to acknowledge his existence until he gets those awful Velociraptor claws fixed. Must be nice to know that if comedy doesn't work out, he can always make a living in Steven Spielberg blockbusters. Or maybe a bit of elective surgery is in order; we can take Don's feet and switch them with Chuck's. That way Don can comfortably enjoy dressing like a Taliban member and Chuck can avoid all of those tiresome stairs and just scale the side of the fucking building.

This is not about Chuck Mignanelli's cowardice, the deformity of Don's feet, or the warm, safe-from-the-Boogey-Man embrace of Kenny. Nor is it about Jim's family, who all look and sound exactly like him, or the erection-inducing odor of Tony's finger. Unfortunately, it's not about Jim's new beard, either (if, in fact, you can refer to it as a beard). I am only calling it that due to location; above the eye it would be considered an eyebrow and under Hitler's nose it would be classified as a mustache. The only advantage to a beard like that is if you run out of shaving cream you can just as easily remove it with a DustBuster.

 You decide; is it a beard or thumbprint on the negative?

This is not about any of these silly things; it's about Jim's birthday celebration and the superb decision to hire Sabbra Cadabra. Named after one of Sabbath's finest and most underrated songs, they not only sound exactly like Sabbath in the early seventies, but they have every behavioral nuance down as well. Joe (Ozzy) has every single facial expression of Ozzy Osbourne including the odd little smiles he gives, as well as the exact hand clapping motion and hand-over-the-ear pose during certain lines. He even holds the mic just like fucking Ozzy, not to mention having two of Ozzy's chest tattoos. He sounds just like Ozzy when he sings, and between songs he screams about alcohol (when he wasn't heckling me and Florentine, which caused us to giggle and clap like schoolgirls). The only true difference is the bulge in the front of Joe's pants. It is, for lack of a better term, awe-inspiring. There is no way Ozzy's cock could be that big. It looks like he has little Connor Peterson stuffed into his boxers. I wonder if girls walk up to him and ask, "Is that a drowned fetus in your pants or are you just happy to see me?"

Patrick Lachman (lead singer of Damageplan) flew in for the party and it was great when Joe took a breather and Patrick sang "Heaven and Hell" with the band. Another fine moment was when he shook Chuck's hand at the end of the night and refused to let go. Chuck doesn't really like to be touched and Patrick held on to his hand for a good ten to twelve minutes. You should have seen the panic in those sultry blue eyes. The only thing that would have made me happier would have been if Patrick was holding Chuck's hand while we all raped him in an elevator. All in all, a fine party.

With Sabbra Cadabra.

YOU GELLIN'?

AS I PREPARE for a nap, I am watching an interesting show on reconstructive surgery and skin expansion techniques for severe burn victims. This show is really amazing me, not to mention throwing a wet blanket over my desire to scrap a load before bedtime. Another case being featured is a woman who lost her eye to cancer. A prosthetic is being made so she can live more normally, without the gaping hole in her face. (Although if I were her husband, I'd discourage the prosthetic and get quite a bit of mileage out of that extra hole. Oh, on your period again, huh? No problemo; take off those glasses, you silly goose.) What impressed me the most, though, was not the burn victims themselves, but their respective spouses. They were being completely supportive and loving; accompanying them to the hospital and to physical therapy, as well as offering encouraging words. Seeing this really drove home the fact that I've never truly been in love. I came to this conclusion because the words they offered were genuine and meaningful, not the halfhearted nonsense I'd spit out. "Hey, look on the bright side; you already have a brown hat, now all you need is a green-and-red-striped sweater for Halloween."

At this point in my life, I am just a tad too shallow about looks to be supportive for long. I'm sure I would be at first; you have to give someone a few days to recover before you dump them. Even I am not a big enough creep to march into intensive care and tell a girl with full face and head bandages that I think we should see other people. At first I'd just cheat; minor indiscretions at work, maybe a quickie in the office or a handjob at lunchtime. Hopefully my conscience wouldn't allow me to start getting blown in the hospital parking lot right away. I know myself well enough to admit that it wouldn't be long before I started using the obvious power shift in the relationship to my own awful advantage. I'd start showing up three hours late without explanation, or start exhibiting passive-aggressive behavior, like commenting on what a controlling cunt her mother is. If she dared to object I'd tell her that we're just too different and leave for a week or so, hoping she'd break up with me. It would probably take more than that, though. I am below-average looking, but once a gal has burns over 90 percent of her body, I suddenly become quite the catch.

This is not intended to shit all over burn victims, by the way. I am simply reporting what an ass I am and how I'd probably behave. Even if I did decide to tough it out and make things work, my self-centeredness would invariably get in the way. It's easy to pretend I don't care what people think, but the base lie in this statement would become obvious through little behavioral subtleties. I'd make inappropriate suggestions like, "Maybe we should move to Alaska or Siberia," hoping she doesn't catch on that these are freezing climates, which would require wearing a ski mask for at least half the year. I'd always walk two steps ahead of her in the mall, and instead of being affectionate, I'd refer to her as buddy or pal when people were around. Going out to eat would be a chore, as I'd always have to call in advance to secure a corner table in a dimly lit part of the restaurant. If she ever confronted me on my horrid and shameful behavior, I'd throw the old "it's not you, it's me" line at her.

She'd know I was lying and her penetrating gaze would size me up through glasses that are taped to the sides of her earless head. Christmas would undoubtedly be a debacle, as her wish list of CDs and perfumes would be ignored, replaced by full wig and beard sets and Elton John–sized sunglasses. She'd start complaining about our sex, which would only consist of me applauding and shouting, "You go, girl!" from across the room while she masturbated on the couch, followed up by high-fives and blowing her a kiss goodnight. If she insisted on staying with me, eventually I'd just dump her for something innocuous, like leaving the cap off the toothpaste or crying in pain while I was trying to watch the Cowboys game.

The people in this program did impress me tremendously, but what prompted me to write this chapter was actually a commercial that was shown while it was on. It starts out with two men standing in the street outside of their cars, which have obviously just been involved in an accident. There is a white man and he has been carelessly rear-ended by a male Negro. There are cars backed up and horns are blaring, yet these two have smiles on their faces. They both realize their oddly good moods and make the connection; the Negro male looks at the white man and asks, "You Gellin'?" and the sellout white coward responds, "Like Magellan!" This in lieu of the appropriate response, which would have been, "I most certainly am not Gellin', you absentminded, careless spook."

"Gellin'" is the term used to describe their fine moods due to the fact they are wearing some sort of Dr. Scholl's massaging gel insoles in their shoes. By now it should be obvious that the *g* in "Gellin'" is a soft one as in "George." If your mind processed the *g* hard as in "get," then please close this book immediately and hang yourself.

The thing that brought such instant rage in me was the fact that this fucking company thinks this is funny advertising and somehow catchy. I suppose the juxtaposition of this idiocy with *Burn Victim Follies* brought out my irritation even more. It wouldn't have been as bad if a man had rearended a woman and asked, "You Gellin'?" and her response was, "No, but my cunt sure is smellin'," or if he asked the same question after running into his stepson's Big Wheel and the lad answered, "Quit touching me at night, or I'm tellin'." Maybe the thing that upset me so much was the fact that the Negro male had struck the hard-working white gentleman. Had the white fellow responsibly asked, "You Gellin'?" the black guy's response of, "Like a watermelon," would have been wholeheartedly amusing and a fine advertising tool.

Considering the seriousness of the show that was on, both fellows in the commercial should have been burn victims. The first man could have asked, "You Gellin'?" and the man whose car he hit could meekly respond, "Actually, no. It's a salve I apply to prevent infections." I understand the importance of the rhyming scheme and would expect this one to be rejected outright by the client.

Incidentally, I have the gel soles in a pair of dress shoes, and they are quite comfortable. The only problem is when I slip on the shoes the insert bunches up in the front of the shoe so I have to reach under my arch and pull it back. I speak from experience when I say that wearing these mushy, gel-filled foot comforters are indeed pleasant, but they don't cause life to become so Utopian that I would forgo vengeance of any sort. They have not prevented me from patronizing hookers, nor have they done anything to alleviate the rotting, sickly sweet odor that wafts out of my belly button.

KONG

I TRIED TO get a set at the Melrose Improv last night, but none were available because it was one of those specialty theme shows I fucking *hate*. This particular abomination was called "Gender Benders," and it was, of course, mostly gay and lesbian comedians. Most comedy clubs have fallen into this repugnant trap and have special nights for Latino, all female, or black comics. Just another example of "don't mention my sexual preference /race /gender unless it benefits me." I flew cross country and needed to work out material to do on Leno, but couldn't get onstage because I don't like to put on a paisley shirt and have my mouth fucked. If I'd have mentioned a few of my transsexual indiscretions, they may have let me do the check spot.

I am yet again on an airplane, heading back to New York, and stretched out in the emergency row like an experienced business traveler. (Except for the fact I'm wearing an *Opie & Anthony* T-shirt and pancake stage makeup like some fucking fruit from the "Gender Bender Ass-Eating Extravaganza.") The two seats on my left are empty, which is very rare and extraordinarily pleasing.

Normally when I fly, I request an aisle seat because my bladder is the size of a hummingbird clit, which causes me to piss constantly. While on the phone booking my Newark to LA leg of the flight, the agent gave me the emergency row aisle seat. A few minutes later I got a message from that agent apologizing and saying that while she and I were talking, some cocksucking sneak of a passenger snatched the seat she had promised me, so now I'd be stuck in the window on a five-and-a-half-hour flight. I was beyond irritated, and in moments like that I wish I had children so I could get out a little frustration by hitting them.

Wednesday morning I boarded the plane and took my shitty window seat. Fifteen minutes later a couple got on to occupy the aisle and middle seat. The wife was a porker and had a body like Mr. Apple in the Fruit of the Loom commercials. Her husband walked a few rows back to put luggage in the overhead, so I took the opportunity to ask her if she'd mind switching to the window and explained my urination habits. I was very grateful when she said yes, this way I wouldn't have to spend forty minutes climbing over her every time I needed to piddle. Her husband came back a few minutes later and sat next to me. He was a Mexican fellow, around 5'11" and not at all fat, just slightly stocky and very tall. He was a bit crammed in his seat and his elbow touched mine a bit, which bugged me. I noticed he had an awful mustache perched over a pair of nice, thick, kissable Mexican man lips. You know the kind I mean? They are fairly juicy, like two pregnant slugs relaxing under a filthy mustache awning.

I was annoyed at having him next to me, especially when I looked at the woman in the aisle seat to my left. She was reading the paper without a care in the world. She and the window seat guy had the middle seat nice and empty between them and she had the paper open with that "there's no one in the seat next to me" confidence. She had on a lime green matching pantsuit, which I *detested*, and her hair and glasses made her look very much like Sally Jesse Raphael. Just a gal in charge, reading the paper, ready to kick a few asses and take a few names. I was jealous of her situation, and began wondering what would happen if I took one of her nicely painted red toenails into my mouth and bit down until she either screamed or neatly folded up her newspaper and swapped seats with me.

As the flight attendants are making final preparations before closing the cabin door, this thing, this fat fucking MONSTER walks down the aisle and stops at her row. I was leaking clear stuff as this 6'5", 350-pound behemoth waited for her to step out so he could get to the middle seat. It was fucking great. This guy looked like Al Roker with blond and black shoulder-length dreadlocks. He unceremoniously plopped down into the seat with the same grace that a fifty-pound bag of cement plops down onto the sidewalk after being hurled off the Empire State Building. His winter coat and big fat arms were halfway in her seat. I honest to God thought it was a woman until the end of the flight. I realized it was a guy when I got a closer look and saw chest hair, and then heard him say his name on the phone. You know you're a fat fuck when people have problems making a gender identification. Nothing could have pleased me more. Mrs. Matching Lime Green Pants Suit Comfortably Reading the Fucking Newspaper was now going to have to fly clear across North America pinned against her armrest by this fat, Hawaiian shirt–wearing, androgynous blob. You have *never* seen someone look so miserable. Rusty Yates sported a happier face when he went to clean the ring around the tub and found baby hair on it. She began sighing loudly like people will do when they're suddenly forced to sit next to a black glacier with dreads. She had to lean almost into the aisle to read her paper, now all cramped up and half open. As the plane took off, she slid down to where her ass was almost off the seat just to try and relax without Sasquatch touching her.

Meanwhile, back at Camp Thick-Lipped Mexican, things were beginning to get annoying. The awful wife who had given me the aisle seat decided she wanted to sleep, so she keeps putting her fat head on her husband's arm. He has his tray down and is doing a word search and she keeps rubbing his arm affectionately. Why do people get married? I could never put up with that shit. If I were him, I'd have started circling words like "CUNT," "DIVORCE," and "ACCIDENTAL DROWNING." The annoying thing was that she had actually positioned one of her horribly overworked, yet muscleless legs on the emergency door. With all of the excess tonnage those gams haul around, I'm sure one casual stretch would have sent that door screaming off the fuselage and into the back tail fin. And as she gets comfortable, she's edging him over so he's now leaning against me. I tried to keep my arm on the armrest, but his skin was extremely warm and it gave me the creeps (not to mention a tent in my sweats). I was not nearly in as bad a shape as the other lady, who by now had given up on sleep and instead just sat slumped in her seat in a rage. By now the guy next to her had fallen into deep slumber and his head lolled back stupidly over the top of the seat. Every time she glanced at that big black arm in her personal space, she must have rooted for the in-flight movie to be *Mississippi Burning*.

Just when I thought it couldn't get any better, he began to snore. It really was amazing that of the six people in both emergency rows, the only two sleeping were the fatsos who were inconveniencing everyone around them. We're all crushed and wide awake and cranky, while these two had inhaled their awful egg and biscuit breakfasts, then hibernated for the rest of the flight. There is absolutely no valid argument against someone as big as the shitbag in the next row paying for two seats on a flight. As much as it made me giggle to see this businesswoman miserable, she should not have to be uncomfortable for more than five hours because of someone else's carbohydrate addiction. The woman in my row was not in the pay-for-two-seats range, although I wouldn't even let someone half her size lick my nipples while I jerked off in the car.

I think my favorite part of the whole experience was the way Businesslady kept glancing over at me in desperation. We were actually bonding over the fact that neither of us was a fat blob of shit. Her eyes said, *Help me*, and in return I'd give her the old *Sorry you're stuck next to a fat silverback* eyebrow raise, then returned my attention to the *Black Inches* magazine I was perusing. At baggage claim in LA, I tried to strike up a chat with her, hoping to score a blowjob. She completely ignored me, as she should have.

I recently found some photos of me from a couple of years ago. The nerve of me to ever criticize someone else's appearance, considering what a fucking chub I was.

Who is this hammy, Curley Joe-looking motherfucker?

MONSTER RAIN

THE MORE I look back on my childhood, the more it becomes apparent that I was an odd little boy. Hyperactive my entire life, shrinks wanted to put me on Ritalin until my mother stepped in and vetoed the idea. She thought it would hurt her little Jimmy's creativity and free spirit. I had many hobbies when I was a youngster, one of which was destroying beehives with rocks. My friends and I would find one and pelt it with bricks until it was ruined and the bees had to abandon it. This practice came to an end when I saw my friend Denny running and screaming because he had three yellow jackets stinging him on his outstretched arm. I also remember my friend Teddy having bees fly up his shirt and sting him repeatedly. I now have a fear of bees that undoubtedly began with one of these stupid instances. Too bad a prostitute didn't sting Denny or young Theodore; perhaps I would have developed a healthy fear of spending half my income on sex with emotionally damaged women.

Recently I told the story of Monster Rain on the air and it's been sweeping the nation ever since. When I was in first or second grade my friend and I would play this fun little game. We would be bored, walking around our apartment complex, and one of us would yell, *"Monster Rain!"* and we would both scamper under the porch to avoid being rained on. While we were under the porch avoiding Monster Rain, we would kill time by blowing each other. I am not sure what the connection was between oral sex and the Monster Rain; hindsight dictates that an umbrella would have been more practical. I am also beginning to doubt that there was any real Monster Rain at all; I now suspect we were using this fictional occurrence just to get under the porch and kiss each other's dingles. I don't even remember the kid's name to be honest, nor do I remember what he looked like. I do, however, remember one time he was wearing Budweiser swim trunks that smelled like mothballs. Just in case you have moments where you think your life sucks, at least you don't have to contend with the memory of kneeling under a porch and sucking the hairless wiener of a boy whose testicles smelled like your grandmother's closet.

The actual porch under which Monster Rain took place. I believe there were shrubs in front of it when I was young (if not, what a dumb, out-in-the-open cocksucker I was). Looking at this photo gives me the creeps; notice the ominous, dank-looking open cellar window.

The trick when playing this game was to get your friend to blow you first. Both parties wanted to be the receiver, not the giver. It was great when my little buddy would lift his embarrassed face out of my lap, ready for his turn, and I'd mumble something about being "late for lunch" and dash out from under the porch. He'd be left with self-loathing and dick breath while

I skipped freely and ratted him out to all of our friends. "He's queer bait, he licked my dingle!" At that age, I was just more comfortable with my little buddies than with girls. Vaginas scared me; I'd see a pussy and think God hadn't finished making her yet. A girl named Janice, who was a year older than me, put her hiney against my face in the woods when I was in third grade and changed my life forever. But I've never forgotten my roots; I may have moved on, but I will not let such an important tradition fall by the wayside.

Three men just laughing, looking for a porch.

I am not sure why the Monster Rain phenomenon is taking the world by storm (pun intended), but it is. When I was in Sacramento, I walked onstage and a group of guys began chanting, "Monster Rain! Monster Rain!" and they had on homemade Monster Rain T-shirts, which gives this movement a very middle-America, grassroots feel to it. I am trying to manufacture portable porches so people all over our nation can just set them up and suck each other's cocks at a moment's notice. Americans and their porches will be like Muslims and their prayer mats; we'll set them up four to five times daily: in traffic, in bank lines, all over this great land. At the Hammerstein Ballroom recently, not only did "Monster Rain" chants break out in front of the venue, but in the middle of one show a fan ran up and threw a Monster Rain hat onstage.

I see this thing becoming as big as baseball. Fathers will teach it to their sons, boys will play with boys from other neighborhoods, and eventually—a professional league. It will be the goal of every red-blooded American lad to have his kneepads placed in the Monster Rain Hall of Fame. I have finally found my ticket to international prestige and respect. I began a revolution, and it all started in Edison, New Jersey, under a porch with a mouth full of shame.

The second best way to avoid getting Monster Rain on you.

LITTLE MISS BIG NIPS

I AM CURRENTLY waiting for a girl to show up so I can pay to suckle her larger than average nipples. I was perusing Craigslist earlier this evening and saw an add for "breast play," which seemed fun and interesting. The gal in the ad claims to have much larger than average nipples so I gave her a jingle and invited her over. Just to be silly I'm going to make loud suckling noises, much like the sounds a St. Bernard makes when lapping chocolate milk out of a dish.

The young lady has come and gone. She was an attractive girl who claimed to be Puerto Rican, although I suspect she was Indian. She wasn't in the door for more than two minutes before I realized this was probably going to stink. I knew she was only allowing breast play, but she wouldn't even go into my bedroom. She looked at the office chair I'm currently sitting in and indicated it would work better if I kept my ass parked in it while she placed her nipples in my mouth. Sucking tits in a office chair sure did sound hot; I was hoping we could then segue into me fingering her asshole while she tallied a few receipts on a Microsoft Excel page. So, I sat there like an idiot while she took off her sweater and bra. And I will say for the record, her breasts were lovely. They were not too large, with very dark, wide areolas that made it look as though her tits were wearing Moe Howard wigs. And the nipples were very long, jutting out like two delicious, suckable hammertoes.

She had the potential to be a very sexy girl; she fed me her nipples and teased me with them while I sat there with my awful head tilted back, mouth open like a baby bird. I suggested we move to the couch so we could be more comfortable (actually, so I could be more comfortable, she could have been standing barefoot in broken glass for all I gave a shit). She knelt on the couch and went back to the old routine and when I rubbed her back she put my hand back on her breast. I rubbed her ass, same thing: back to the breast. I asked her to just touch my nipple and she said no. I almost told her to get out, but since there are no refunds I figured there was no need to bite off my nose just to spite my face (especially since by biting my nose I was preventing semen from being shot all over myself). So I continued suckling like a baby lamb and bag wacking until I splooged all over my Sabbath shirt. This prompted Ms. Sex-Appeal-of-a-Drunk-Driving-Accident to put her bra and awful sweater back on, but not before asking me if I'd like to "clean her off." I guess that's supposed to be a part of the sexy fantasy; not only can I tug my mule while she does nothing, I get to wipe my saliva off her tits when I'm done! Old civil rights footage flashed in my head and I'd have given ten years of my life to be in possession of a fire hose.

Her fee was a hundred bucks and this idiot actually looked hurt I didn't tip her. She can take her hurt feelings and plunger nipples and go jump in a lake. Maybe if the breast-feeding business doesn't take off, she can open a restaurant called Cook It Yourself, Motherfucker.

AN UNEVENTFUL, SHITTY NIGHT IN BOSTON

I DROVE UP to Boston with Opie on Thursday afternoon because he and Ant had a television interview. We had a leisurely drive up, grinning, making eye contact, and enjoying some New England foliage together.

I mention the foliage because about four years ago I was booked to do a college with Colin Quinn and Keith Robinson. I wanted to go up the night before and sleep all day, but stupid Colin wanted to drive up to see the foliage. I was fucking miserable waking up early for a three-and-a-half-hour drive so this asshole could look at some colored leaves. Keith was an hour late as usual (I realize it's not his fault, it's a melanin thing), and as we headed up I realized that Colin wanted to drive during the day because his driving is too horrendous to be trusted at night. What a fucking old lady he drives like. I would have felt safer with Harry Chapin behind the wheel. I screamed at him for the entire trip, which simultaneously made me feel better and ruined any enjoyment he may have taken from the picturesque landscape. At one point we're in the left lane and a truck in the *center* lane slowed down, so panicky Colin applied his brakes and I really blasted him. "What the fuck are you slowing down for? He's not in the same lane as you stupid. Jesus Christ, you really suck at this." I felt immeasurable joy racing through my veins every time I let him have an earful.

He admitted some time later that I did indeed ruin his trip completely, and instead of feeling guilty I felt giddy and vindicated. Coincidentally, he is up here in Boston this weekend performing at the Comedy Connection. I won't get to see him but I smile at the thought of good ol' Col on his way home, stopping in the shoulder to place some colorful leaves in his fall scrapbook, and being rendered legless by a drunken teenager joyriding in a stolen car.

Driving up on Thursday, Op and I stopped at a few rest areas, some because we needed to and some just to stand at the urinal and do a little man-to-man peeking. Every time he pissed I followed him right in and stood at the urinal directly next to him no matter how many were empty and available. I'm sure people in the bathroom thought we were a couple of vacationing fruits. On a one to ten scale in the world of rest area men's room cruising, I'm a three and Opie is an eleven.

As soon as we got to the hotel I shit for so long my legs felt numb, then crashed for a few hours while Op and Ant went to do their interview. We met up with Ben and Steve for dinner, as well as two hot chicks. One of the chicks was an XM employee; therefore I couldn't hit on her. Her friend, however, was a cute blonde who did not work for XM. Unfortunately, she looked at me like I was Michael Landon's pancreas; therefore I couldn't hit on her, either. We had a nice dinner and then went bowling. I haven't bowled in years (except for that time I went in Columbine LOLOLOL TRENCH COAT MAFIA ROTF K-MART LOLOLOL). I forgot how awful bowling shoes are; red on one side and green on the other. It shouldn't even be called bowling, it should be called "roll a ball while sporting the footwear of a Puerto Rican." I wound up scoring a ninety-five or so, not bad if you're four years old or Bob Dole.

We all pretty much stunk, especially Steve C. He has big, thick foreign fingers, which must be wonderful for digital penetration, but are atrocious for bowling. His fat toe-fingers wouldn't fit in the ball so this clod is just half rolling, half shot putting the ball. It would *thud* about two feet in front of him and then roll into the gutter. I was up right after him so I think his beyond-awful skill level gave me the confidence to be all I could be. I left after one game because I was tired and had a ferocious urge to masturbate.

Once back at the hotel I drained my little Irish bag of all life-giving seeds and then ordered food and ate candy from the mini bar. I have been eating relatively well and I have no idea why I suddenly had the urge to jerk off and sugar binge.

After taking a disgusted look at my belly I decided to stop already and rent *Spider-Man 2* on SpectraVision. It was very good, although I wish Tobey Maguire would have left his mask on a bit more; I didn't need to be reminded of how boyishly handsome he is every three fucking minutes. The guy who played Doc Ock was great and he looked like the Dr. Octopus I remembered from the comic books. Am I the only one who notices that Doc Ock, when said quickly, sounds like Da Cock? And if I'm not, please tell me I'm not the only who has pointed out that phonetics trick to a seven-year-old while rubbing his frightened tummy. Let's hope the third installation is finished sooner rather than later. I have it on good authority that Spidey battles AIDS in the next one, using his web to clog the cock holes of villains just before they drop a batch of tainted cake batter into the mouth or eyes of an unsuspecting citizen.

I woke up Friday afternoon around three, had a quick lunch, and then took a shit that resembled a paintball accident. After showering and shaving, I headed down to the lobby to meet Op, Ant, Steve, and Club Soda Kenny. As we're all standing in the lobby waiting for Ant, Kenny bellows loudly, "Attention, ladies and gentlemen of the Omni Parker House Hotel, attention please." Of course everyone shut up and looked, as there was a 6'5" weirdo with a gay porno mustache demanding their attention. He continued, and I quote, "The time is now exactly 5:20 p.m. Thank you." And that was the end of the big announcement.

We walked to the Big Easy for the event, stopping at two different Starbucks so I could purchase the infamous iced lattes with soymilk. In the spirit of rebellion, I refuse to talk in Starbucks-speak. I will not now or ever ask for an "iced grande soy latte." I am an American and I drink mediums, not grandes. I also don't like the order they say the words in. Grande iced latte with soymilk should be the way it's said (and yes, I am only saying "grande" now for the sake of the discussion). Reversing the words and mixing them up isn't hip or avant-garde, it's irritating. Starbucks employees sound like Yoda when they bark the orders out. You don't ask a girl to "asshole your fist" while she's sucking your cock, do you? Reversing words is communistic and I'd rather be dead than red. Anyway, after I downed my second of these powerful yet tasty beverages, all remaining materials in my colon threatened to stage a jailbreak.

I had to take my shit at the venue, which sucked, because while I'm hovering over a piss-covered toilet seat I hear two of our asshole listeners talking. One of them blurts out that he can't believe, "how fucking fat Norton got." I hated this prick not only for his rudeness, but also for his honesty and accurate eyesight.

One thing I never get sick of at *O&A* events is seeing tits, simply because there are normally about ten total combined breasts at any of our given get-togethers. We did have a few very nice WOWings, with one hot girl even asking me to sign the swell of her bosoms. I got NOTHING, as usual. Even promises of fame and bellies full of alcohol couldn't persuade one of these lovelies to let little Jimmikins piston his prick in and out of their shitters. The closest I came was pressing my erection into the crotch of a girl who had a 6.0 blood alcohol level while she was standing against a railing. I am thirty-six years old and I'm trying to hump a stranger like a Great Dane. I kept leaning in to speak and grinding my boner on her crotch. I thought I was doing well until I stood back and she toppled over to the left and almost hit the floor. If I'd have realized she was that drunk I never would have pressed against her like that; I would have skipped all the small talk and deep-dicked her in a bathroom stall while she vomited.

THE TWO-FOOT RULE

LAST NIGHT WE were chatting with a guy who was the DJ in a local strip club. I very rarely go to them because they bore me and leave me wanting. I prefer to skip the chatter and go straight to an escort. But I wanted to do something since it was our final night in Boston. There was absolutely nothing going on, and I confirmed the only shot at sex I had was raping Kenny's mustache.

Since the titty bar was only a few blocks from the hotel I decided to walk. On my way there I made a wrong turn and strolled onto the set of a John Singleton movie. Part of me thought I should not be a racist and just walk down the block, yet another side of me realized that being a racist beats a razor slash to the face. Thankfully, bigotry prevailed and I turned around quickly. I found the place a few minutes later and was ushered up to the VIP area where Anthony, Big Kev, and Kenny were. The girls were very hot, totally naked, and hopefully up for taking a donation to do the Electric Slide over my face.

They were serving alcohol, which was odd with total nudity. In Jersey, totally nude clubs are only allowed to serve nonalcoholic beverages. There's nothing quite like staring up into a cavernous twat while sipping a chilled carrot juice with your buddies. I realized how this club got away with it when I glanced over and watched a guy getting a lap dance. Apparently, strip clubs in Boston have this horrible "two-foot rule." This means that the dancers have to remain at least *two feet away* from customers while dancing for them. How sexy. During a lap dance, you always want a gap the size of a tractor trailer between you and the cocktease who's entertaining you.

The four of us sat there aimlessly chitchatting, with Ant occasionally throwing balled-up dollar bills over the glass partition and down onto the stage. I didn't throw anything but I gladly would have if there'd have been a Molotov cocktail available. I finally decided to try a table dance (even that's an inaccurate description; "vicinity dance" is more like it) because I had to see for myself how awful it was. The bouncer, an Asian gentleman who made up for in muscles what he undoubtedly lacked in genitals, sat me on a chair, broke out his compass, and pointed where the lady would be standing to give me my dance. This distance thing would be okay if the club provided the patrons with bushes to put on our laps so at least we could jerk off and pretend we're spying on the girls.

She began her dance, which might have been fairly hot if she was within shouting range. The dance really started to stink when she sat in the chair in front of me, opened her legs, and I couldn't see her pussy. It's the first time I've ever needed binoculars in a strip club. Feeling this girl's tits would have been considered getting to second base because they were ninety feet away. Fucking Boston. There's horrendous traffic due to the fact that these idiots decided to install a tunnel the length of the city, and going to a totally nude strip club has all the eroticism of a Motor Vehicles inspection.

I don't know why I love that goddamn city so much. Maybe because, as a general rule, the girls only require a pint of Guinness to fuck, despite my awful luck these last two days. Or maybe it's because Charles Steward shot his preggo wife and then himself, blamed it on a black guy, and the whole fucking city bought it without question. Or, maybe it's because the last two assassinated public officials in America came from there. Who knows and who gives a hoot. Despite awful strip clubs and traffic and rampant racism, Boston is A-OK with me.

YUCK MOUTH

ONE MAJOR PROBLEM I have with most comedy writing is the obsession with making the characters likeable. It's not the likeable part I hate, it's the non-threatening, faggoty interpretation of what likeable is. On most shows it means you do a little good-natured ribbing, get a scolding, and finally learn a lesson at the end of the episode. It's this unspoken rule in Hollywood that has hindered the creation of my own sitcom, which has been ready for production since 2000. The working title of my show is *Yuck Mouth* and revolves around the trials and tribulations of Terry, a male nurse whose spaghetti obsession causes his mouth to constantly be filled with the bile brought up from acid reflux burps. Terry is the everyman; 6'8", 400 pounds, and trying to reacclimate into society after doing seventeen years for a string of robbery/rapes. The potential for merriment is virtually endless.

The pilot begins with Terry's release from prison. He walks out into a sunlit afternoon, throws his arms open to breathe in the fresh air, then promptly trips and falls down (to add to the humor, sound effects will be used; you will hear a loud *BOING* every time Terry takes a tumble or induces a miscarriage with a battering ram). Due to physical restraints, I obviously will not be playing the lead. In addition to being very large, Terry has a beard, which he keeps to hide the eczema that covers half his face and 80 percent of his torso. He habitually bites his fingernails down to the soft pink skin, so he has to scratch his itchy beard with pens, car keys, and butter knives.

There is a very funny and surprisingly touching scene in episode three when Terry is having breakfast at a roadside diner called Hitler's Eats. The meal is a substantial one: two sow belly omelets with a turnip juice chaser and a bedpan full of buttery grits. He is trying to flirt with the waitress while unconsciously scraping a fork back and forth through his beard. She notices the skin flakes covering the countertop and quips, "Ya autta scrape yer face over a baggie; we could cut it with baby powdah and sell it to the Mexicans." Terry pounds his fists onto the countertop as he howls with laughter. The waitress (whose name, according to the tag on her uniform, is Millie-Jo), curiously studies this large, jovial creature sporting dandruff in his beard, flaky red ears, with bloody diapers hanging from his coat pocket. In mid-laugh he bursts into tears over his condition, and we are left to ponder this man's agony as he weeps softly into his grits while Millie cleans the counter with a DustBuster.

I have two possible endings for this episode; in the first, Terry and Millie-Jo become involved in a short-term relationship. Her eleven children have taken to Terry after only one brief, alcohol-fueled molestation. They want him to move in, but the idea of having an instant family scares him after so many years alone in prison. Instead of facing his fear, Terry bakes them a chocolate cake laced with rat poison and hops a midnight bus to Shreveport. Most people who have read this version felt depressed by it and much preferred the alternate ending, which had Terry and Millie-Jo breaking down while driving to the premier of a bestiality film Terry produced. He tells her to check the engine while he stays in the truck and masturbates to Japanamation photos he carries in his wallet. Suddenly there is an explosion, and Millie-Jo is horribly disfigured with third-degree burns over 98 percent of her head and face. Seeing her smoldering with no hair or eyelids, Terry mumbles, "Holy Toledo" and attempts to hitch a ride to Beverly Hills, where he feels he'll fit in.

Due to a series of wacky events and misidentifications, Terry becomes the mayor of Beverly Hills and proceeds to wreak havoc. He tries to get a bunch of nutty laws passed, such as Mandatory Blowjob Tuesdays and having all nonwhites summarily executed. The Beverly Hills scenes very well may need to be rewritten, as networks have historically been squeamish about genocide humor in sitcoms.

The news for Millie-Jo turns out brighter than originally expected. While in the burn unit she meets Dr. Tubbs, a world-renowned skin specialist and amateur magician. Working under the name Colostomy the Magnificent, he has spent years toiling fruitlessly in seedy lounges and doing midnight shows in turnpike rest areas. His act consists mainly of making Go Fish! cards disappear and attempting sleight-of-hand with cinderblocks and AIDS needles.

After removing the anus skin of a cadaver, he stretches it and grafts it over Millie-Jo's head and face. She is horrified by the results, and notices that whenever she blinks, her toes raise in unison. And due to sloppy hole cutting, the eye lines in the skin are too low so she is now legally blind. She is too embarrassed to complain, though; she's grateful to Dr. Tubbs for keeping her entertained at night with mediocre card tricks and Polack jokes.

Dr. Tubbs's medical license is revoked when an orderly walks in on him and Millie-Jo having sex one night (more like just him, as she was unconscious thanks to a morphine drip and *Laverne & Shirley* marathon). She is thrown out of the hospital for being such a deep sleeper, so out of desperation, they cling to each other. Millie-Jo becomes his magician's assistant, and they go out on the road together as Turtlehead and Tubbs.

The mysterious stabbing death of the only other contestant gives them first prize in an amateur magic competition. It's unfortunate, though, because second prize was a *Tonight Show* appearance, and first prize turned out to be a Ziploc Baggie of Doug Henning's ass hair. They try to make lemons out of lemonade and weave Millie-Jo a miniscule wig from their prize. She now finds herself constantly being mauled by dogs and hit on by homosexuals who are attracted by the scent of her wig.

I'm stating the obvious, but there is comedic gold in these characters. My end goal is to somehow tie Terry in with Dr. Tubbs and Millie-Jo in some sort of light-hearted postapocalyptic scenario. I realize I've only given you a thirstwetting taste, so stay tuned . . .

MEAN GENE THE HUGGING MACHINE

OF ALL THE people I've looked up to and hero worshiped in my fantasy-fueled life, none have been there longer than Kiss. My earliest fantasies revolved around them. For many of my childhood years, I had this bizarre ritual of not letting myself shit. I'd literally hold it for hours and kneel by the side of my bed in a prayerlike position. I could never sit down when I was holding a dump, it would hurt my stomach. Some psychologist said that holding in logs is some odd form of sexual pleasure, but my thoughts were never sexual. Well, I shouldn't say never; that was around the age I was running around blowing the whole neighborhood under the Monster Rain porch.

The Kiss fantasy was a particularly weird one; I used to daydream about them coming to my apartment in their makeup and costumes, beating me and hurting me and throwing me violently down the steps. Then when I was at the bottom of the steps wounded and crying, they'd hug me and love me and make it all better. I have no idea how that translates psychologically, however, I suspect the end result is forking over cash after blowjobs.

One of my first more-than-passing encounters with an idol was going to be interviewing Gene Simmons with Op and Ant back on WNEW. I pretty much sat stoically while they interviewed him, and then they called me out and told me to ask him something already (he had already scolded me because my chair was squeaking while he was pontificating about life, love, and the advantages of marketing Kiss ad nauseam). I went blank like an asshole and couldn't think of a question on the spot, so I finally blurted out, "So, how is Star Stowe doing?" Star was a former Playboy model who did a famous photo shoot with Gene on a chopper and I'd heard that they dated after that. When I said her name, the guys didn't know who she was and thought it was a joke, so they laughed. Gene thought I was making fun of her, so he said, "That's not funny; unfortunately, she passed away." Fantastic! The one fucking question I come up with pisses him off and offends him. I felt like a complete shithead.

This Hallmark card was taken after at WNEW. It's one of my favorite pictures.

Fast-forward almost three years and we have since been thrown off the air and are back on again. We do a phone interview with Gene on XM. After he hangs up the listeners are *killing* him, saying he's a greedy asshole and I'm defending him the way a codependent makes excuses for a spouse who gets drunk and belly-punches everyone in the family. A couple of weeks after our phone interview, I see him out in Vegas walking into a men's room. I lurk outside the bathroom and say hello, telling him I'm on

O&A and we just interviewed him. I asked for a photo and he was very dismissive, saying he didn't have time, but I could walk with him and take one if I wanted. So I did and he completely ignored me, refusing to stop. This after knowing I had just interviewed him. I was devastated, to say the least. One of only four men who I ever wanted to beat me up had basically just told me to go fuck myself. I went completely ballistic on the air two days later and figured that was the end of the saga. Not quite.

Approximately six months later I am asked to be a judge for Philly radio station WYSP's annual Babefest. It's a bikini competition that draws a huge crowd and I had hosted it the year before. I agreed to be a judge, hoping one of the strippers would blow me for a favorable vote. Well, lo and behold, who is hosting it this year? You guessed it, smartypants: Gene Simmons. I saw him backstage and said hello, he was very friendly and had absolutely no memory of ever meeting me. We were chatting amicably and I was pleased as punch. He was friendly and relaxed and we talked about the Middle East. I even handed him a copy of my second CD (irritating, I know), hoping he'd give it a listen. I wasn't angry anymore and in true spineless amoeba fashion, I just prattled on with him and neglected to mention anything, including the on-air lambasting he received from me. My internal conflict with Gene was over without him ever having known about it.

The contest begins and I'm introduced with the other judges—Jim Florentine, Bam from MTV, and one of the Philadelphia Eagles. A star-studded panel, if there ever was one. It's at the Electric Factory in Philly and the place is packed, three thousand animals with shitty Pennsylvania accents. Gene is finally introduced and the crowd goes apeshit, and the entire thing is being filmed for his reality show. Suddenly he starts addressing one specific person in the crowd, asking him if he wants to be on television. Gene invites this guy onstage and he's so anxious to get up there he almost kills himself when he breaks a fluorescent light on his chest trying to jump onto the stage. I assume he's just an overzealous Kiss fan doing the same thing I'd be doing, which is acting like a complete ass to get close to Gene.

The eager lad finally makes it onto the stage, he says something to Gene and then begins walking toward me, pointing. In one, horrifying instant I realize what's going on; he's not a Kiss fan, he's an *OPIE & ANTHONY PEST.* Impending doom hits me in the face as this fucking maniac takes the mic from Gene and starts screaming, "I want to know why you wouldn't take a picture with Little Jimmy Norton in Las Vegas?? Did you think you were too good to take a picture with Little Jimmy?" I was mortified. Gene took the mic back from this psycho and walks over to me on the sofa, actually *grabs me by the hand,* and gently walks me to the middle of the stage. He has no goddamn idea what's happening, only that there is a major problem occurring and it has something to do with me.

Babefest is literally two minutes old and I am standing in the middle of the stage in front of three thousand people holding hands with Gene Simmons. Into the mic he asks me, very tentatively, what I would like to happen right now? I felt like a mammoth asshole and on top of the world at the same time. I say I'd like a picture together, please. He puts his arm around me and proceeds to hug me for the picture. He even raises his leg and I hug back for dear life. In the midst of all this discomfort and in front of a mob of cheering alcoholics, I am, after thirty years, finally getting my hug from Gene Simmons.

Backstage he approaches me and fills me in on what had happened. Apparently when he was first walking out and waving at the crowd, this kid is center stage in the audience jamming his middle finger up in the air screaming, "FUCK YOU, GENE! FUCK YOU!" To squash the problem, Gene called him up onstage to try and diffuse a potentially ugly situation.

Gene then asked why this nut would ever have thought that he had wronged me? I had to sheepishly explain the Vegas photo incident and I mentioned that I "casually brought it up on the air" and that the fans are a bit overprotective. I neglected to mention the fact that I was screaming on the radio wishing him any and all diseases a person can catch via their cock. My moment of truth had arrived, and I weaseled and soft-stepped around it. I am truly a yellow-bellied shitdick.

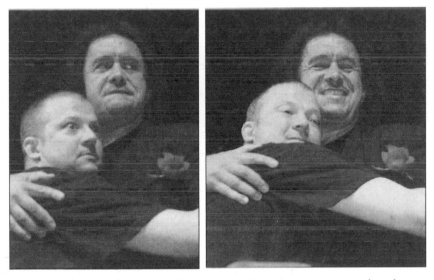

It just doesn't get any better than this. It just doesn't get any creepier than this.

At the end of the night we said our good-byes and he asked me, with sincerity, "We're okay now, right? Is everything fine?" I truthfully informed him that everything was indeed Jim-fucking-dandy.

I've seen Gene a couple of times since then, most recently when he came in studio for an interview. He remembered me and was friendly. There's an old song Kiss did called "Goin' Blind" and it has a very odd line in it, "I'm 93, you're 16 . . . and I think I'm goin' blind." Wondering what that line means had been driving me nuts, so I asked him about it as he left the studio. He had to run through the song real quick in his head, so he started singing it as we're walking down the hallway. I realized that not only did I get my hug from Gene, he was now softly serenading me. He told me what the line meant—nothing, just a silly line Paul Stanley had come up with—and we said our good-byes.

A few weeks later we had Paul in studio promoting his solo record. He was very laid-back, talked about banging chicks and being on the road and how Ace Frehley is trying to sober up. Opie made me tell him my childhood fantasy of the band throwing me down the stairs and hugging me. I plowed through it and tried not to think about what an absolute asshole I must sound like. He took it in stride though, and we chatted up a storm walking from Free FM over to XM. A nice-sized crowd had gathered and was following us, and at the end of the walk, Opie suggests to Paul that he hug me. At that moment I think he'd have preferred to hug a wolverine with AIDS, but the crowd cheered and he agreed. We had a nice hug on Fifty-seventh Street.

As for the Babefest pest, Club Soda Kenny removed him from the stage before things got out of hand. (After our hugging picture, the kid started screaming at Gene again, demanding an apology for "making Little Jimmy Norton walk alongside him and not taking the picture." Special-interest groups are less interested in apologies than this fucker was.) I pulled Kenny aside and made sure he wouldn't be thrown out, and he wasn't. That fucking lunatic *screamed* at a rock icon in front of thousands of people because he knew my feelings had been hurt. I'll always love that pest; it's the nicest thing a fan has ever done for me. And of course, I'll always love Gene, Paul, Peter, and Ace. Two hugs down, two to go.

ROACHES FOR THE BEST MAN

THUS FAR, MY LA trip has been an irritating disaster. I was busy in New York and unable to get out here to apartment hunt, so my managers told me they'd find me a suitable place. I needed a furnished place fairly close to West Hollywood so I don't get stuck in hours of LA highway traffic. They found me some lovely digs about six blocks from the Improv, which is about ten minutes from here. Perfect. I got into town, picked up the keys, and headed to the place, laughing and beeping and waving at passersby, just a generally sweet, happy boy who'd come to Hollywood to make good.

Upon entering the apartment, I realized it was livable, but slightly teetering on shithouse. I unpacked my belongings and attempted to hook up the DSL for my computer so I could quickly download things I would need for work, such as rape videos and hidden toilet cam footage. Of course I had trouble connecting to the Internet. Of course I couldn't do it. Nice to know that my technical fucking retardation had followed me across the country like a vomit-colored shadow. Yoshi picked me up in his horrible car (people always stare when we go by. They were obviously wondering what a fancy man such as myself was doing in such a lowly vehicle) and we headed over to the Improv.

I say hello to some people I haven't seen in a while and continually drop words like "studio" and "call time" so they know I'm out here working. Hours later I allow Yoshi the honor of dropping me off. Being it was my first day here I tolerated his unsightly clunk box; from now on he'll have to steal a newer model car if he wishes to enjoy my company.

I enter my new West Coast pad and flip on the lights. I notice a "thing" scampering across my doorway. *"This better not be a fucking roach,"* I not only think but say aloud. Closer examination reveals that it is indeed a roach, running quickly with those fucking disgusting, probing, icky cockroach antennae out in front of it. I take off my shoe and smash it, figuring this unfortunate shit-wallower just learned a tough lesson about whose apartment to stay the fuck out of. I then do a quick scan of the walls and floor, as any reasonable fellow would. I am just about to give myself the mental "all-clear" sign when I notice a slight movement in the kitchen against the baseboard. I intuitively realize that if this isn't a piece of blowing dust I might have a major problem on my hands. You have undoubtedly surmised that it indeed was not dust, or else I wouldn't be writing this paragraph. It was another dirty, filthy roach. Two roaches on exact opposite sides of the apartment does not bode well for the "wandered in accidentally" theory.

I grabbed my camera and walked back into the dining room/kitchen area and noticed about seven more of the invasive little fuckers. I started taking pictures and short camera videos so the landlord couldn't claim I was lying. Most of the roaches were pretty small; I finally saw a nice-sized model when I opened one of the cabinet doors and it stared me down before sauntering away. I knew I'd have to move out quickly; as I've stated many times, I am a fancy man, bordering on gentleman. I packed up my crap after grabbing enough footage to start my own offshoot Discovery Channel and then headed into the bedroom. I figured I'd grab a few hours' sleep and then head out in the morning. That was a fantastic idea until I saw a roach on the bedroom wall. I am not a roach expert but when you see one in the bedroom with the lights on, you are fucking infested. I killed it and promptly saw another one on the bedroom rug, so I immediately started calling hotels for a room RIGHT NOW.

I didn't need this skin-crawling shit at this hour. I was tired and just wanted to kick back in bed and lazily penetrate my asshole with a yellow highlighter pen. And of course, I couldn't find a goddamn hotel; they were all booked because of the upcoming Emmys, so I called my manager in a rage at 2:30 a.m. and he worked his magic and found me a place for the night. I grabbed my suitcase, laptop, duffel bag, and two large boxes of clothes and headed out the door. All of this at 3:00 a.m., while hobbling on a badly injured foot.

One of the more irritating aspects of this sudden upheaval was that two days after arriving in LA I was scheduled to fly to Edmonton, Canada, for Rich Vos's wedding. I was his best man so I was sort of obligated to be there. I was supposed to be settled and unpacked; instead I was in a small hotel room with all of these dumb possessions and nowhere to put them. And the fact that this dummy had to get married in Edmonton really made me want to decapitate him. There is *no* convenient way to get there. Continental has more direct flights to Karachi than they do to this shithole. I booked a flight from LA through Minneapolis then up to Canada on Northwest. (My other options were Air Canada and Alaska Air. I'd sooner mail myself in a FedEx box then get on either one of these airlines, ever.)

It was a nine-hour trip each way because of the three-hour layovers. I spent every moment in that awful Minneapolis airport fantasizing about bashing Rich's brains in with a paperweight.

The wedding was held there because Bonnie's family lives three hours north of Edmonton, and it was the closest city with an airport (they live on a farm somewhere in the mid 1850s). We stayed in the same place that the ceremony and reception were to be held at—a hunting motel that her aunt runs. I highly recommend this, as nothing adds to the romance of a wedding like a man in filthy boots standing in the middle of the lobby with a gunnysack full of deer intestines. I was glad to be there, though,

Some fucking retard, myself, and Keith Robinson in 1995.

and hanging with Rich and Bonnie took my mind off the enraging living situation in LA.

Apparently it's traditional that the groom gives the best man a gift (more of a payoff so you don't yell, "Don't do this, you dumb motherfucker!" in the middle of the ceremony.) He gave me a beautiful Tanagro watch. It really is nice (worth $2,500 according to subtle, classy Rich Vos). This watch was one of the gifts from the Oscar gift basket he got writing for Chris Rock last year, which was filled with a lot of expensive gift cards and offers. (He's lucky the baskets didn't reflect good material actually contributed, or his would have contained two prosthetic cocks and a Swatch.)

We met the following afternoon around 1:00 p.m. to have the wedding photos taken. Six of us squeezed into a minivan and drove through scenic Edmonton. We pulled into a rest area, which was great, I had to piss. Instead of everyone waiting in the van, they all got out and walked over to a woman holding a camera and tripod. With horror I realized that the wedding photos were going to be taken *in the rest area*. We walked to a large lawn behind it and began posing near a tree. I was only in a couple of the photos so I had plenty of time to run inside and drill a buddy-hole between two stalls.

Women have probably never seen them but on the road in some truck stops there really are awful little holes that men will use to peek through. To jerk off on a toilet is hard enough; to do it while also pressing your face against the metal wall of a rest room stall peeking through a dime-sized hole has got to be a feat of modern physics. Personally I need to lie on my back when I jerk off and my feet have to be pointed straight out and straining, not unlike Christ on the cross. I'd also love to know who is bringing a drill into a men's room with the sole purpose of peeking at a cock. I can't decide if it's disgustingly creepy or admirably dedicated. And how do these guys not get caught? I've never noticed an outlet near the toilet, which means these sexual sociopaths are undoubtedly plugging an extension cord in somewhere. What kind of award-winning performance do you have to pull off if a state trooper walks in at four in the morning while you're kneeling in the men's room dripping pre-cum and operating power tools?

If I was tinkling and saw a man doing remodeling work just to catch a gander at my hog, I'd probably show it to the fellow on principle. "Go on, take a good look, Ace, you've earned it." I'd also like to see a beer ad campaign dedicated to these living-in-the-shadows craftsmen. "For all of you shame-filled, closeted married men who 'run out to the store' every night and come home hours later with North American trucker semen matted in your hair—this Bud's for you."

The ceremony went off without a hitch, marred only by dumb Rich's inability to repeat what the (I don't know what her title is, the lady who did the nuptials. She looked like Bea Arthur, and I kind of wanted to play with her tits.) read to him. He was a nervous, mush-mouthed horse's ass and we all silently felt pity and revulsion for him. The reception was nice;

I sat there with my bum foot stretched out and watched Bonnie's family gather around the bar and collectively do an amazing Robert Downey Jr. impression. Apparently one of the guests was so loaded he shit his pants on the dance floor. Let me repeat that: *A man shit his pants on the dance floor at a wedding reception.* He went to his room, hosed himself off, came back out, and continued boogeying. And that man, in his moment of sulking realization as he gingerly stiff-legged off the dance floor with a mocha log in his sock, still handled himself with more grace and dignity than Rich trying to repeat the wedding vows.

Now this anonymous, shut-eyed dumbbell is wrecking my photo with Chappelle.

It's been over two weeks since the wedding and I attended the LA version of the reception a couple of days ago. *Enough already*—I am SICK of the goddamn wedding. They get married in Canada, fly to New York for a party, they're working on getting a reality show picked up, fly to the West Coast for the LA party; who the fuck do these two creeps think they are, Charles and Diana? Someone needs to sit Rich down and explain that he's not a "man about town." He's a lonely, frightened zilch who somehow batted out of his league and duped a hot girl into marrying him. His idea of class is applying wood varnish to an end table he picked up at a yard sale, and yet this cocksucker is running around like he's on the cover of this month's *Cigar Aficionado*.

And I finally found an apartment. I wasted two grand in a hotel and then found out the thieving *cunt* who rented me the roach-infested apartment is trying to give back less than $300 on an $1,800 deposit. I'd love to chop off her deposit-stealing hands and yank my cock with them. Her argument is that she held the apartment for the weeks before I got to LA. I'd love to explain to this *pig* that the fact that she knowingly rented a roach-infested apartment makes everything null and fucking void. I hope this greedy bitch finds a tumor on her ovaries the size of a medicine ball. Or even worse, I hope she hooks up with Rich Vos after Bonnie finally dumps him.

ACKNOWLEDGMENTS

This book would not have been possible without:

My parents, I owe it all to them. Thanks, Mom and Dad, for fucking sometime in October of 1967. And thank you to whatever vehicle I was conceived in.

My sister Tracy and nephew Nick for actually admitting they're related to the slob who wrote this drivel.

Gregg Hughes, the actor who plays Opie, and Anthony Cumia, the actor who green-screens himself into World War II Nazi footage. I've never enjoyed anything as much as doing the show with you two. Correction: I've never enjoyed anything that does not end with a load on my stomach as much as doing the show with you two.

Colin Quinn, because *Tough Crowd* made me a better writer and a better comic. Not to mention that your encouragement of my writing gave me more confidence in it than anyone else's could have.

My managers and agents, who stuck by me when we were kicked off the radio and kept me working: Pete Papalardo and Dennis Arfa, everyone at AGI, David Steinberg, Jonathan Brandstein, Larry Brezner, and everyone else at MBST; as well as Robert Eatman and everyone at Robert Eatman Enterprises You're great, loyal friends; I have no idea what you're doing in the entertainment industry.

Lydia Wills, my book agent who, despite my snotty, leaky nose, continued pushing me until I finally wrote this.

Tricia Boczkowski, my editor. Thanks for holding my hand through this process; I realize I have no idea what I'm doing. *And I'm sorry I overused italics.*

Jen Bergstrom, for taking a chance on me; I hope I don't sell ten copies and get you fired.

Jack Romanos, for approving the money—prostitutes all over the tristate area thank you.

Club Soda Kenny, for being my road manager and friend, and for reminding me that I shouldn't smile too much, as a frown is probably right around the corner.

My loving girlfriend. I feel like I was dead before I met you. Now, I only wish I was.

This book would have been very possible, but not as much fun, without:

Bob Kelly, I'd love to rebreak your fucking knee. Keith Robinson, Patrice Oneal, Rich Vos, Bill Burr: I have no idea why I like any of you. The *Opie & Anthony* crew: Steve Carlesi, Roland, Derek, Than, Travis, Danny, Sam, E-Rock, Bill, Keith the Cop, Mike Cole, Jack, Ron and Fez, and especially Earl Douglas, for making my photo with Black Sabbath possible. Big Kev for his riveting interviews, Twitchels, Big A, No Filter Paul and Denise, Dugout Doug, Debbie Wolf, Lucci, Silly Goose on Cam, Pat from Moonachie, Cara and Eddie, all of the Pests, anyone who has ever helped me scrap a load on Paltalk, F.B.A.com, Wackbag.com, and CringeHumor.net, especially Patrick. Eric Logan's barber, Don Wickland, Master Po, Mars, Will Chapman, Lee Abrams, and Jaime Cologne from XM Satellite radio. John Mainelli, Tom Chiusano, Mark Chernoff, Lisa Orban, Jodi Salidore, Alllll, and everyone else from CBS radio. The brilliant Rob Bartlett—hang in there, angel. The Comedy Cellar (Este, Noam, Ava, Yeela, Hatem), Caroline's on Broadway (Caroline Hirsch, Andrew Fox, and Louis Faranda), Vinny and Vicky Brand and the Stress Factory in New Brunswick, The Comedy Connection in Boston, Stand Up New York, The Comic Strip, The Melrose Improv, Yoshi, Joey Silvera, Evil Angel for providing an endless amount of masturbation fodder, Michelle Arnold, Eric McMahon, Don Jamieson, Jim Florentine, Bobby "the cock" Levy, Otto Peterson, Ariel Nemiroff, Marina Franklin, Geno Bisconte, Arde Fuqua, Eddie Trunk, Jeff Ross, and KC Armstrong. Paul Fishbein, Gary Miller and Mark Stone from AVN, and Jessica Drake for being such a great cohost for the AVN Awards. Jeff Gordon, Geoff Wills of Live Nation—thanks for being so good to me with all the gigs. Dr. Steve, Erica Stone, Kevin Chiarmonte, Chelsea & Rufus Peretti, Pugs & Kelly, Sarah and No-Name, The Sports Junkies, Barry Katz, David Letterman, Eddie Brill, and Eric & Justin Stangel.

Louie C.K., Pam Adlon, Rick Shapiro, Mike Haggerty, Laura Kitlinger, Jerry Minor, Kim Hawthorne, Kelly Gould—my fellow cast members on *Lucky Louie*. We deserved season two. Also Andrew Weyman, Mike Royce, Bob Krakower, and the rest of the behind the scenes crew from *Lucky Louie*; thanks for making something out of my sub-mediocre acting. From HBO: Caroline Strauss, Chris Albrect, Nancy Geller, Nina Rosenstein, and Tracy Katzky—by the time this comes out I'll have shot my one hour special; let's hope I didn't suck.

Jay Leno, for always putting me on the couch with women who wouldn't dream of sleeping with me; Ross Mark; Bob Reed; John Melendez and the entire *Tonight Show* staff. Thanks for being so good to me.